# The
# Downloader's
# Companion
## for Windows™

Scott Meyers

Catherine Pinch

Prentice Hall PTR

Englewood Cliffs, New Jersey 07632

*Library of Congress Cataloging-in-Publication Data*

*Editorial/Production Supervision:* Lisa Iarkowski
*Interior Design:* Gail Cocker-Bogusz
*Acquisitions Editor:* Mary Franz
*Manufacturing Manager:* Alexis R. Heydt
*Cover Design: Whitman Studios*
*Cover "Wizard" Illustration:* Gail Cocker-Bogusz

The publisher offers discounts on this book when ordered in bulk quantities. For more information, contact:

Corporate Sales Department,
Prentice Hall PTR, 113 Sylvan Avenue,
Englewood Cliffs, NJ 07632, Phone: 800-382-3419,
FAX: 201-592-2249, E-mail: dan_rush@prenhall.com

Printed in the United States of America

10 9 8 7 6 5 4 3 2 1

ISBN 0-13-342254-2

Prentice-Hall International (UK) Limited, London
Prentice-Hall of Australia Pty. Limited, Sydney
Prentice-Hall of Canada, Inc., Toronto
Prentice-Hall Hispanoamericana S.A., Mexico
Prentice-Hall of India Private Limited, New Delhi
Prentice-Hall of Japan, Inc., Tokyo
Simon & Schuster Asia Pte. Ltd., Singapore
Editora Prentice-Hall do Brasil, Ltda., Rio de Janeiro

*For Nancy, who moved,*
*even though she didn't want to.*

— Scott Meyers

*For my parents, Dave and Dorothea Pinch,*
*who provided unconditional love*
*and acceptance for my entire life, no matter*
*what. And for Mike, who has no idea*
*how special he is.*

— Catherine Pinch

# Contents

# Acknowledgments

There are many people we'd like to thank for their help with this book. First, a heartfelt thanks to those who painstakingly reviewed drafts of the manuscript. Their honesty, insight, expertise, and willingness to adhere to unreasonable schedules helped improve the text in innumerable ways. Our reviewers were Julie Blumenfeld, Laura Craighead, David Hiers, Walter Howe, Tim Johnson, Fred Kush, Douglas Meyers, Vivian Neou, Thomas Powell, Grayson Silaski, and Nancy L. Urbano. Of course, we bear responsibility for the shortcomings in the book that inevitably remain.

We are also indebted to the authors of the software included with this book. They have been generous with not only their programs, but also with their time. When we mined the riches of the Net, these people and their products turned out to be pure gold. The authors are Leonardo Haddad Loureiro (LView Pro), Robert Jung (ARJ), Nico Mak (WinZip), Bill Neisius (WPLAny), Bruce Sabalaskey (Xferpro), Dean Thomas (Odometer), Xing Technology Corporation (MPEGView), and Haruyasu Yoshizaki (LHA).

We are grateful to Dan Doernberg for his comments, suggestions, and guidance at a time when this book was little more than an idea. We are also grateful to Erick Hammersmark, who selflessly brought WPLAny to our attention and thereby eliminated his own fine sound-playing program, PlayNow, from the list of programs we included with the book.

Scott Meyers has these additional acknowledgments: I am, as always, indebted to my wife, Nancy L. Urbano, who not only put up with my long hours at the keyboard, she also endured my incessant book-related chatter during the months this project absorbed. Her patience continues to astonish me. I am also pleased to acknowledge the generosity of those members of the Net who came to my aid when I was first struggling to learn Windows. Without the sage advice of Bob Desinger, Clifford Dibble, David Hall, Jeff Fishbein, Peter Goudswaard, Julie Melbin, Jeff Morris, Stephen Posey, Gary Rumble, and Philip Taylor, I'd *still* be trying to figure out how to save my desktop setup.

Catherine has these additional acknowledgments: I'd like to thank the people who have spent their time and efforts (and sometimes frustration) in training and coaching me in various areas of my life, both in and out of the computer industry. A few of these are Yutaka Yaguchi, Janet Bush, Marcia McClocklin, and Jill Wooldridge. There are many more than I can list here, but you all know who you are and you have my deepest gratitude and thanks. A special thanks to my ex-roommate, Sheryl Berovic, who bore with my moods during the writing of this book, and didn't complain when she had to do more than her share of the house-cleaning.

# About the Authors

**Scott Meyers** has a Ph.D. in Computer Science from Brown University and is the author of the best-selling *Effective C++* (Addison-Wesley, 1992). An internationally recognized authority on C++ software development, he provides consulting services to clients worldwide.

**Catherine Pinch** has been involved in the field of Computer Science for 12 years, working in programming, documentation, and other areas. She currently owns her own company and provides technical documentation services, including consulting, analysis, and writing for software products and companies. In addition, she has a black belt in Karate and competes regularly in the United States and other countries.

# Introduction

How would you feel if you went on a trip around the world, brought back a collection of gifts and souvenirs, and then found you couldn't unpack them? What if you were expected to figure out what was inside each package just by looking at the wrapping? What would it be like if you knew what was in each package, but you couldn't unwrap them anyway?

## A Cornucopia of Chaos

This is the situation in which many online travelers find themselves today. There are treasures galore waiting to be picked up online, regardless of whether you connect to a bulletin board system (BBS), an online service like CompuServe, or the Internet. You'll find software, much of which is better and virtually all of which is cheaper than that proffered by your local software store. You'll find files containing documents — even entire books — online. Pictures, sounds, and movies — these, too, are available to you in untold abundance when you start exploring the online world.

But there is a Catch-22. Yes, you can get the online software, but that software is in a format you can't use without more software, and the only way to get that additional software is to go online again and get it, which requires that you already have it. Furthermore, the instructions on how to run the software are also in an inaccessible format. Yes, the online world is filled with treasures, but in many ways they always seem to lie just out of reach.

## This Book and The Net

This book provides the information you need to make use of the multitude of files you can get from what we call *the Net*. The Net is whatever computer or computers your PC talks to, typically through a modem over a telephone line. The Net includes CompuServe, America Online, Prodigy, GEnie, and the other commercial online services that have been springing up like mushrooms after a heavy rain. The Net also includes the Internet, that vast network of interconnected computers that spans the globe and is used by over 25 million people. The Net includes the thousands of BBS systems that cater to all imaginable tastes and interests. Simply put, if it's a computer and your computer can connect to it, it's part of the Net (see Figure 1).

Our aim in this book is to provide the icing on the networking cake. You've heard about what's available on the Net; maybe you have even copied — *downloaded* — some of the Net's files to your computer. Now you want to know what you've got, what it's good for, and how you can use it. This book will tell you.

We provide the tools you need to open your new-found treasures. We describe how files on the Net are named, we tell you how to predict their contents, and we explain how you can run programs, view image files, listen to sound files, and otherwise enjoy the fruits of your digital travels. Most important, we get you out of the Catch-22 by providing the software you need to do these things.

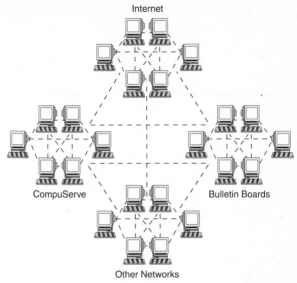

Internet

CompuServe

Bulletin Boards

Other Networks

Figure 1

## The Structure of This Book

Including this introduction, there are seven chapters in this book, each of which deals with a specific aspect of downloading. At the end of the book are two appendices and an index. Accompanying the book is a diskette containing some of the best software on the planet Earth.

**Chapter 2** explains the concepts of freeware and shareware, which together comprise not only the most common types of software found on the Net; they are also the most useful. In addition, they are a compelling reason for becoming adept at downloading in the first place. Authors of freeware and shareware are consistently more innovative, more responsive, and more concerned about quality than the corporate behemoths who dominate the software industry, and the fruits of their labors are one of the greatest treasures of the Net. All the programs that accompany this book were culled from the Net, and all are freeware or shareware.

**Chapter 3** covers the nuts and bolts of downloading. After examining the basic ideas, we move on to meatier subjects: how file types and version numbers are embedded in Net file names, how to avoid downloading outdated files, how to go about choosing a file transfer protocol, how to configure your phone line when dialing in to the Net, how to guard against becoming infected by Net-borne computer viruses, how to avoid corrupting files when moving them between other computers and your PC, and how to tell the File Manager about the meanings of new types of files you've downloaded.

**Chapter 4** describes how files are usually stored on the Net. There are thousands — possibly millions — of downloadable files on the Net, and, if left in their original form, they would quickly swamp the available disk space. As a result, they are *compressed*: made smaller without losing any data. Even if disk space were not a problem (and it always is), the sheer number of files would still lead to chaos, or at least *more* chaos, because there would be no way to figure out which files belong together. That problem is solved by *archiving*: bundling related files together. In Chapter 4, we explain everything you need to know about recognizing and working with compressed files and file archives.

**Chapter 5** describes the process of *encoding* that must be used to send many types of files through electronic mail or to post them to bulletin boards. It also explains how you, as a downloader, are affected, and it shows how working with encoded files can be a breeze.

**Chapter 6** describes the multimedia aspects of downloading. It is increasingly common to use PCs as multimedia machines, where programs make use of sounds, pictures, even movies. Unfortunately, there are several ways of representing the data making up the pictures, sounds, and movies, and the representational Tower of Babel that results yields downloading headaches by the bushel. In this chapter we describe the challenges of working with multimedia files, and we show you how to overcome them.

**Chapter 7** contains a carefully selected list of recommended books that discuss topics of interest to downloaders, including going and being online, archiving and compression programs, sound players, and picture-displaying programs. It also mentions two of the largest and most useful software repositories on the Internet, and we explain how you can purchase CD-ROM copies of the files they contain, even if you don't have access to the Internet.

Finally, **Appendices A and B** summarize the meanings of more than a hundred file extensions you may encounter in your travels through the Netosphere.

## Icons in the Text

We use the following icons to call special attention to particularly important information in this book:

We use this *installation* icon whenever we describe how to install one or more programs that are on the book's diskette.

We use this *wizard* icon whenever we have important advice to give you. When you see this icon, you can be sure the information nearby is especially worthwhile. Think of the wizard as the voice of experience.

We use this *pitfall* icon to point out places where it's easy to go wrong in one way or another. Follow the advice near the icon, and save yourself needless grief.

## *The Software*

What with downloadable files being compressed, archived, and encoded in a bevy of different ways and with the data they contain being represented in enough different formats to make even the most hardened of Netmeisters cry Uncle, it should be clear that you can't really get started as a serious downloader without a well-stocked arsenal of programs to handle the requisite unarchiving, uncompressing, decoding, and representation-understanding. Unfortunately, you won't have much luck procuring the necessary software at your local software retailer, because many of the programs are, as they say in late-night television ads, *unavailable in any store*; they have to be downloaded from the Net itself. Which puts you in an interesting position: in order to download the riches to be mined from the Net, you have to be able to download from the Net.

In truth, however, that is not the biggest hurdle you must overcome. More daunting than figuring out how to download the programs you need to download is this: figuring out which of the multitude of available programs are the ones you really want. To take but a single example, when we last checked a popular Net program repository, we found over a dozen programs that act as Windows interfaces to the DOS archiving program called PKZip. You surely want such an interface, because a good one (such as WinZip, which we've included with this book) is worth its weight in gold, but the only way to figure out which one is best is to download each one, learn how to use it, then give it a try. That's not only time-consuming; it's laborious, tedious, and — if you're paying for each minute you spend downloading — expensive.

 Fortunately, you can forget about such drudgery, because we've already put in the online legwork for you. Included with this book is a veritable dream team of software for the downloader. After evaluating hundreds of programs, we chose the following stellar performers for inclusion with this book:

- **WinZip**, **LHA**, and **ARJ**: These are programs that handle the most common archive formats in the world of DOS and Windows. With these programs installed, you can download virtually any kind of DOS or Windows software, and you won't have to waste time or lose sleep worrying about the precise format the software was in before you downloaded it.

- **XferPro**: The most common ways of encoding files for movement through electronic mail or bulletin boards are uuencoding and xxencoding, and Xfer-Pro manipulates such files quickly, easily, and automatically. It also handles MIME-encoded files, which are becoming increasingly common. Most other programs that decode these kinds of files make you use DOS at least some of the time, but we would never ask you to do something like that; XferPro is a Windows program through and through.

- **LView Pro**: The Pro means professional, and this program is most certainly that. Not only will it let you view pictures stored in any of the four most common picture representation formats, it will also let you edit those pictures in more ways than you can imagine. But although it's powerful enough to satisfy even the most finicky PC graphics professionals, it's also simple enough for people like us to use.

- **WPLAny**: If your PC has a sound board, you won't know how you lived without this program. WPLAny makes it possible for you to double-click on almost any kind of sound file and hear the sounds contained within. Unlike many competing programs, WPLAny understands that sounds are meant to be heard and not seen: it doesn't take up any valuable screen space when you use it. Of course, that alone wouldn't earn it a place in our book, but the fact that it recognizes five different sound file formats does.

- **MPEGView**: Movies on your PC? Of course, but you have to have the right software to view them. MPEGView is that software. With it installed, all you have to do is download the movie, double-click on the file, and break out the popcorn.

This collection of software would be a bargain at any price, but one of the things that makes it especially attractive is that most of the programs are *free*. As long as you're not using them for commercial purposes, you'll never be asked to pay a penny for LHA, ARJ, LView Pro, WPLAny, or MPEGView. Try finding a deal like *that* at your local software dealer.

WinZip and XferPro, on the other hand, are shareware, so you're obliged to send in the registration fee for those programs if, after evaluating them for a reasonable period of time, you decide to keep them. Even so, the two of them together cost less than forty dollars, which is an astonishingly good deal for programs of their utility, quality, and professionalism.

Frankly, the software that comes with this book is, in and of itself, worth much more than the price of the book and diskette combined. We hope you'll pardon us for bragging, but it really is a great deal.

## Sample Files

We've also included some sample files that allow you to try out these programs without having to search the vastness of the Net for suitable data. Wanna try your hand at exploring the contents of a file archive? We've got several. Feel like decoding an encoded file? We have one. Perhaps watching a movie is closer to your idea of entertainment? There's one on the diskette. How about listening to recorded sounds or looking at color pictures? Those, too, you'll find included on the diskette that comes with this book.

## Late-Breaking Software Information

Several weeks go by between the time a book is completed and the time it finally appears in print. A lot can happen in several weeks, however, especially in the world of software, where products may be updated every few months. As a result, we've included a file called *readme.txt* on the diskette that accompanies this book, and you should read that file to find out the latest information about the software that comes with *The Downloader's Companion*.

## *Installation Summary (For the Impatient)*

 In the chapters that follow, we explain how to install and use each of the programs that comes with this book, but perhaps you're the kind of person who likes to install first and ask questions later. If so, you should appreciate the following installation summary, which briefly describes how to install all the software that accompanies this book. If you get stuck during the process of installing a particular program, just turn to the part of the book that gives a more detailed description of how to install that program.

You will need about 2.6 megabytes of free disk space to install all the programs that come with this book. You'll need about 320 kilobytes more to install all the samples on the book's diskette. Installing everything will therefore require about 3 megabytes of free disk space.

1.  **Create directories**: Create the following directories on your hard disk:

    c:\arj
    c:\lha
    c:\lviewpro
    c:\mpegview
    c:\winzip
    c:\wplany
    c:\xferpro

    You will also need a directory where you can put temporary files. Many people use the directory *c:\temp* for this purpose, and in the instructions that follow, we assume that's the directory you use. If *c:\temp* doesn't already exist, create it, too.

2. **Install ARJ**: From the *programs* directory of the diskette that comes with this book, copy *arj241a.exe* into the *c:\arj* directory you created. In the File Manager, double-click on *c:\arj\arj241a.exe* to run the program. When it's done executing, you'll have several new files in the *arj* directory, including *arj.exe*, which is the ARJ program itself; press F5 to make the File Manager update itself and show you the new files. Delete *c:\arj\arj241a.exe* — you no longer need this file.

3. **Install LHA**: From the *programs* directory of the diskette that comes with this book, copy *lha213.exe* into the *c:\lha* directory you created. In the File Manager, double-click on *c:\lha-\lha213.exe* to run it. When it's done executing, you'll have several new files in the *lha* directory, including *lha.exe*, which is the LHA program itself; press F5 to make the File Manager update itself and show you the new files. Delete *c:\lha\lha213.exe*.

4. **Install WinZip**: From the *programs* directory of the diskette, copy *winzip5b.exe* into the *c:\winzip* directory you created. In the File Manager, double-click on *c:\winzip\winzip5b.exe* to run it. When it's done executing, you'll have several new files in the *winzip* directory, including *winzip.exe*, which is the WinZip program itself; press F5 to make the File Manager update itself and show you the new files.

Double-click on *winzip.exe* to run the program. After being asked to acknowledge its features and license agreement, you will be presented with a dialog box for specifying program locations. For ARJ, fill in *c:\arj\arj.exe*, and for LHA, fill in *c:\lha\lha.exe*; then click on **OK**. You will then be asked if you wish to add WinZip to the Accessories group of the Program Manager; we recommend you answer **Yes**. Finally, you may be asked if you want File Manager associations to be set up. If you are, click on **Yes**.

You will then be presented with the main WinZip window. From the **Options** Menu, select **Directories...**, and in the *Default Extract Directory* section of the resulting dialog box, click on "Open Archive Directory," then on **OK**.

Exit WinZip. Delete c:\winzip\winzip5b.exe.

5. **Install LView Pro**: From the *programs* directory of the diskette, copy *lviewp18.zip* into *c:\temp*. In the File Manager, double-click on *c:\temp-\lviewp18.zip* file to run WinZip on it. In WinZip, click on **CheckOut** to bring up the CheckOut dialog box. Specify *c:\lviewpro* for the *Directory* field, then click on **OK**. When WinZip finishes extracting the files from the archive and creates the Program Manager group for LView Pro, exit WinZip by selecting **Exit** from its **File** menu. Click on **No** when it asks you if you want to delete the CheckOut directory and Program Manager group. Finally, delete *c:\temp\lviewp18.zip*.

6. **Install MPEGView**: From the *programs* directory of the diskette, copy *mpegvu.zip* into *c:\temp*. In the File Manager, double-click on *c:\temp-\mpegvu.zip* file to run WinZip on it. In WinZip, click on **CheckOut** to bring up the CheckOut dialog box. Specify *c:\mpegview* for the *Directory* field, then click on **OK**. When WinZip finishes extracting the files from the archive and creates the Program Manager group for MPEGView, exit WinZip by selecting **Exit** from its **File** menu. Click on **No** when it asks you if you want to delete the CheckOut directory and Program Manager group. Finally, delete *c:\lviewpro\mpegvu.zip*.

7. **Install WPLAny**: (This step is useful to you only if your PC has a sound board. If you have no sound board, skip this step.)

   From the *programs* directory of the diskette, copy *wplny09c.zip* into *c:\temp*. In the File Manager, double-click on *c:\temp\wplny09c.zip* file to run WinZip on it. In WinZip, click on **CheckOut** to bring up the CheckOut dialog box. Specify *c:\wplany* for the *Directory* field, then click on **OK**. When WinZip finishes extracting the files from the archive and creates the Program Manager group for WPLAny, exit WinZip by selecting **Exit** from its **File** menu. Click on **No** when it asks you if you want to delete the Check-Out directory and Program Manager group. Finally, delete *c:\wplany\wplny09c.zip*.

8. **Install XferPro**: From the *programs* directory of the diskette, copy *xferp100.zip* into the *c:\temp* directory you created. In the File Manager, double-click on *c:\temp\xferp100.zip* to run WinZip on it. In WinZip, click on **Extract** to bring up the File Extraction dialog box. In the *Extract To* box, enter *c:\temp* (you *do not* want to extract the files to *c:\xferpro*), then click on **Extract** again to extract all the files. Exit WinZip.

   Use the File Manager to double-click on *c:\temp\setup.exe*; this will run XferPro's Setup program. When Setup asks you for the drive and directory where it should make the installation, specify *c:\xferpro*, then click on **Install**. When Setup asks what Program Manager group to put XferPro in, specify the group of your choice or use the default group Setup suggests. When Setup is finished, delete the XferPro files that were copied into *c:\temp*.

9. **Set up File Manager associations**: Set up the following associations in the File Manager. (If you

don't know how to set up file associations, Chapter 3 of this book will tell you, as will the online help for the File Manager.)

- .*gif*, .*jpg*, .*bmp*, and .*tga* files should all run *c:\lviewpro\lviewp18.exe*.

- .*mpg* files should run *c:\mpegview\dmfw.exe*.

- .*uue*, .*uu*, .*xxe*, .*xx*, and .*mme* files should all run *c:\xferpro\xferpro.exe*.

- .*wav*, .*voc*, .*snd*, .*au*, and .*iff* files should all run *c:\wplany\wplany.exe*. This won't do you any good unless you have a sound card in your PC, so it's not worth setting up these associations unless you have a sound card.

That's all there is to it. Your PC will now know how to handle the three most common file archiving and compression formats, the four most common formats for pictures, the five most common sound formats, the three most common encoding formats, and the most common movie format encountered on the Net. Fortunately, you don't need to know anything about these formats; all you have to do is use the File Manager to double-click on files. If a file you double-click on is in one of the formats handled by the programs you just installed, the appropriate program will automatically be run. You can experiment with your new programs by double-clicking on the various files in the *samples* directory of the diskette that comes with this book, because together they will exercise almost all of your new software.

## Getting in Touch with Us

We've done our best to tell you everything you need to know about downloading, but we're aware that even our best efforts are far from perfect. If you know of a way in which *The Downloader's Companion* could be improved, we want to hear from you. Perhaps you think we should have covered a topic you don't find in this book, or you think our treatment of a topic that is in the book is confusing, inadequate, or incomplete. *Tell us.* Maybe you know of better software for accomplishing one or more of the tasks we discuss, or possibly you think we should include additional software to attack a problem we overlooked. *Let us know.* Perhaps you found an error in this book. If so, regardless of whether the error is technical, grammatical, typographical, or otherwise, *please bring it to our attention.* (Don't be shy about this. After all, an error's an error, no matter how small.)

By the way, we're happy to hear from you even if you have nice things to say about the book. In fact, we're *eager* to hear from you if you have nice things to say about the book. Either way, you can send us electronic mail at

```
download@prenhall.com
```

If you aren't able to send electronic mail to Internet addresses, or if you just enjoy the time-honored act of putting pen to paper (or paper to printer), you can send us a good old-fashioned letter:

> Scott Meyers and Catherine Pinch
> c/o Mary Franz
> Professional Technical Reference Division
> Prentice Hall
> 113 Sylvan Avenue, Rte. 9W
> Englewood Cliffs, NJ 07632

We hope you enjoy *The Downloader's Companion*, and we look forward to hearing from you.

# Freeware
# and
# Shareware

All the software provided with this book is either *freeware* or *shareware*. You may not be familiar with these terms, so we thought you should know a little more about what it is you're getting.

## Freeware

Freeware is software you can use with no requirement for payment. It is written by programmers who are interested in providing a service, promoting another product, or who want to have fun with something they do for a living anyway. Sometimes they just want to share a nifty little program with others. There are probably many reasons why programmers make freeware available, but the basic idea is that you are under no obligation to pay for it.

However, the fact that a program is freeware does not necessarily mean you have the right to use it in any way you like. Freeware programs are still copyrighted and owned by their authors, and authors may set distribution restrictions or other qualifications on use of their freeware. For example, we had to get permission from each of the freeware authors whose programs are included with this book.

Sometimes programs will be freeware for personal use, but the author charges a fee for commercial use. The image-viewing program LView Pro, which we've included with this book, is an example of such a program.

 You can tell that software you've downloaded from the Net is freeware by looking at the documentation that typically accompanies it. If the documentation says it's freeware, well, it's freeware. If it says nothing about paying for it, we blithely assume the program is freeware. Thousands of programs on the Net are freeware programs.

## Shareware

Shareware is software that is typically made available through non-commercial channels, but that you are still required to register and pay for. It has been around as a commodity for years, but until recently was relatively unknown, since there is little marketing, no glossy magazine ads, and no television commercials promoting shareware. With the recent upsurge in popularity of the Net, however, shareware is beginning to come into its own as viable, high-quality, inexpensive software. It's a unique situation where the little guys successfully bucked the system. Shareware has become an institution that by its nature depends on ingenuity and creativity over marketing and public relations.

The best part about shareware is that you get to try it before you buy it. You can download shareware, install it on your computer, run it and evaluate it for the duration of a specified trial period, then either send in your registration (and fee) or remove the program from your disk.

## Shareware versus Traditional Software

When you buy commercial software from a standard outlet such as a computer store, you pay for advertising, packaging, shelf space, and other costs incurred during the production, sales, and distribution of the product. The software companies that write and distribute commercial software shell out big bucks just to bring their product to your attention. A quarter-page advertisement in a computer magazine, for example, costs thousands of dollars. These companies invest in graphic designers, consultants, production, and materials to create that oh-so-attractive packaging. It costs thousands more for companies to display their products in retail outlets. And all those costs are subsequently reflected in the price of the software.

Shareware, on the other hand, tends to be created by individuals or companies with a good idea, a solution to a problem, and a small budget. It is distributed through free access media such as the Net or a disk handed to you by a friend or an associate. It is primarily marketed through word of mouth, although bulletin boards will publish shareware reviews, and occasionally a computer magazine also comes out with a review of shareware programs. For the most part, however, the word about shareware is spread by the people using it.

## Benefits of Shareware

 The idea behind the distribution of shareware is that when you get a copy of the shareware program, you take it for an extended test drive, run it through its paces, and make sure it fits your needs. Then, if you like it and intend to use it, you send in your registration and fee. If not, you get rid of the program. The whole system is based on trust, integrity, and honesty. In fact, this is probably the only retail arena where your word as a customer is so valued. This concept works because people do register their shareware and pay the registration fee. If they didn't, shareware would soon become a thing of the past.

You might ask, what are the benefits of shareware, really? For one thing, it's environmentally friendly. After all, if you can download it from the Net, you don't have to get into your car, use fossil fuels to drive to the local computer store to find it, then drive back. You also don't have all that packaging to dispose of. Nothing to landfill, nothing to recycle. The computer industry isn't always the most environmentally friendly of industries, but in this area, it doesn't degrade the environment in any way.

Shareware often provides capabilities you can't find at a retail store. Shareware programs tend to fill a niche that would not necessarily be profitable for big companies distributing software through more conventional means. Such companies gravitate toward supplying big software packages that cover a lot of ground. They look to sell financial/spreadsheet/word processor/business management/wash-the-car-and-dog packages that lots and lots of people will buy. They don't want to spend time and money developing small programs that help a (relatively) few people solve specific problems.

Although it's hard to lump shareware developers into one category or another because shareware itself is so varied, we can say that shareware developers often *are* interested in providing for niche markets. Most shareware programs are very specific, performing one well-defined task and performing it well. There are thousands of shareware programs doing all kinds of interesting things, and as long as there are independent programmers who perceive a problem and do their best to solve it, there will continually be more and different shareware and freeware developed.

We have compiled the following list to give you an inkling of the vast array of shareware (and freeware) available:

- Programs to improve or replace Windows' Program Manager or File Manager
- Viewers and editors for pictures and movies
- Players and editors for sound files
- Programs to display the time: locally, around the world, and beyond
- Programs to calculate almost anything
- Screen savers and wallpaper patterns
- Utilities to organize you, your life, your projects
- Fonts, text editors, and other word processing add-ons
- Communications programs
- Games of every conceivable type

An interesting feature of the shareware industry is that once you have located one program to perform a task, you will often find other programs that do the same task. This is because shareware programs that perform similar functions are generally grouped together on the Net like merchandise at a grocery store. Thus, you might find a shareware program you have been longing to try and suddenly find that the same Net location has ten or more other programs that do the same or similar tasks. This allows you to conveniently try out several programs to compare their relative benefits before choosing which one you want to buy.

As a rule, shareware is inexpensive, typically only about $15-$50 per program, and it's usually closer to $15 than to $50. After all, when you take away the costs of marketing, packaging, shelf space, and all the other expenses that are ultimately passed on to consumers of conventional software, you're left with a good product that is far less expensive than its traditional commercial counterparts.

Shareware as a whole is creative, innovative, and fun. If you can't find what you're looking for in the stores, try shareware. Better yet, try looking for it in shareware first. You will often find great software at a great price.

## Locating Shareware and Freeware

There are thousands of shareware and freeware programs available in hundreds of locations on the Net, not to mention on the computers around you. CompuServe, America Online, Prodigy, other online services, and the Internet all have lots of software for downloading. If you're a bulletin board user, your BBS probably has downloadable software, too.

Getting shareware from the Net is a major reason for going online. If you have access to the Internet, be sure to check out the CICA and SIMTEL software repositories, both of which are described at the end of Chapter 7. Otherwise, check the documentation for whatever part of the Net you connect to to find out where to look for online software. Also, take a look at the books we recommend in Chapter 7, because they describe hundreds of specific Net locations where you can find freeware and shareware to do just about anything.

## Registering Your Shareware

The thing that keeps shareware authors going is the fact that their users register their copies of the shareware. If they didn't, we would probably lose a good number of shareware authors to the commercial market. When you register, everyone comes out ahead. You get high-quality software at a really good price, and the shareware author reaps the financial rewards that encourage him or her to upgrade existing programs and to develop new ones.

And there's more. Registering your shareware typically entitles you to receive more complete documentation, sometimes in hardcopy (paper) form. Usually,
you will be sent the current version of the shareware
on diskette, since the copy you originally downloaded
may be out of date.

When you run unregistered shareware, you'll see that
it's common for such programs to find a way to remind
you to register. They may pop up a message at invoca-
tion, display a banner while you're using the program
showing that the program is not yet registered, or otherwise remind you that you haven't registered. Registered
versions of the software remove these nagging messages.
(Unregistered shareware is sometimes referred to as
"nagware.")

Sometimes the unregistered version of a product has
deliberately limited functionality. Such programs come
with a complete set of documentation, but a small number of the program's commands are restricted or disabled. For example, we know of a shareware program
for playing music CDs on a PC's CD-ROM drive, and the
unregistered version of that program refuses to build CD
databases for more than about a dozen CDs. (Such databases are useful, because they allow the PC to automatically display the songs on a CD when that CD is placed
in the CD-ROM drive.) The registered version of the program contains no such limitation. Shareware programs
that limit the functionality of their unregistered version
are often known as "crippleware." Needless to say, you
get the full-power versions when you register.

You will find that shareware authors tend to be much
more attentive to their customers than big software companies. Shareware authors generally respond to customers' suggestions by making changes for the next release
of software, and bugs are often fixed with exceptional
speed — *days* after they've been reported, not months.
Some authors notify registered users of upgrades and
new releases, and sometimes they even send upgrades to

their customers gratis or for a very small fee. They may invite their customers to suggest improvements they would like to see. Often, registering gives you the right to ask for technical support with the product: the authors can give tips on how to use their programs and can help if you run into trouble trying to use them.

We have provided the information you need to register the shareware that comes with this book. For the shareware you get from the Net yourself, however, you'll need to know how and where to register. Shareware programs are usually bundled with other files, typically text files that tell you how to register your copy and what the requested fee is. These are easy enough to read: just use Notepad or another editor that can read text files. Shareware programs may also display a message giving you registration information when you launch the programs.

Shareware programs generally specify a trial period, usually about a month in length, after which you're required to either register the program or remove it from your disk. You are obliged to abide by the terms of a shareware program's trial agreement, so when a program's trial period is up, make sure you either register that program or remove it from your PC.

## Shareware and This Book

Each program that comes with this book is in its complete and original shareware or freeware form. Don't feel you have to register every shareware program we have supplied with this book. However, you *are* obliged to register your copy of each of the programs that you decide to keep and use. The bottom line here is simple: **If you find yourself using the shareware obtained from this book or from anywhere else, *register it.***

# The Nuts and Bolts of Downloading

One of the best things about going online is that you can transfer files from other computers to your own. *Downloading* is the common term for transferring a file from a far computer to a near computer (see Figure 2). Naturally enough, the term for sending files in the opposite direction is *uploading*. In general, the computer that is farther away is thought of as "higher" than the nearer computer. That's why moving files from the Net to your PC is considered downloading.

In this chapter we give you a computer's eye view of what happens when you download files. We explain what a transfer protocol is and why it's important to you, and we summarize the advantages and disadvantages of the most common protocols available. We then discuss a number of basic issues that every downloader must master. These include how to prepare your phone line for a session with the Net, how to identify the most recent versions of downloadable programs, how to avoid infection from Net-borne computer viruses, and how to tell Windows' File Manager about new types of files you've successfully downloaded.

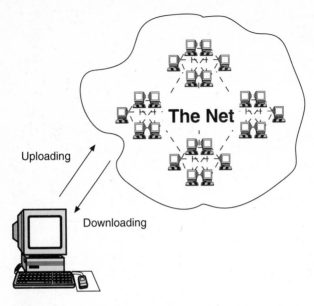

Figure 2

## The Process of Downloading

Transferring files from one computer to another via a phone line involves some coordination between the two computers. A *transfer protocol* defines how the process is to be handled on both the sending computer and the receiving computer.

For the sending computer, the protocol describes how the file being sent should be broken up into pieces, known as *packets*, for transmission. The computer sends these packets along the phone line to the receiving computer (see Figure 3). The receiving computer gets the packets, and, because it is running a program for receiving files that obeys the same protocol, it knows how to reassemble the packets into the original file.

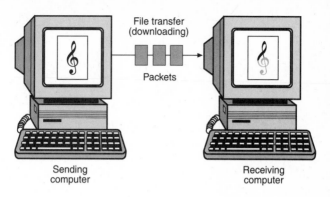

File transfer
(downloading)

Packets

Sending
computer

Receiving
computer

Figure 3

## Error Checking and Transfer Speed

Static and other problems can affect the quality of phone lines, so transfer protocols specify how to check for lost or corrupted data during a file transfer. When an error is detected by the sending or receiving computer, the transfer protocol specifies how the error is to be eliminated. Generally, the lost or corrupted packets are resent. As a downloader, what you want is the fastest possible transfer rate with the smallest possible chance of errors occurring. In general, the bigger the packets, the faster the transfer rate, but the trickier the error checking.

No single transfer protocol always yields the best performance. Some protocols lead to rapid file transfers on phone lines that are "clean" (i.e., have minimal static or other interference on them), but they perform very poorly on noisier connections, because they have to resend a lot of packets. Other protocols lead to slower file transfers on clean phone lines, but they don't need to resend as much data on noisy lines. As a result, you may find you will spend less time waiting for a file to download if you use a protocol that is known more for its tolerance of noise than its speed. On the other hand, if your phone line isn't very noisy, you may decide to put the modem to the metal and go for the fastest protocol you can get your hands on.

There are a number of different transfer protocols in widespread use, and in many cases you'll be forced to choose between them each time you download something. The following sections briefly describe the most common protocols, as well as their advantages and disadvantages. Afterwards, we tell you how to determine which protocol is best for you.

## KERMIT

KERMIT, developed by Frank da Cruz and a legion of Net-based collaborators around the world, was designed to transfer files between all types of computer systems, including between different types of computers and between computers running different operating systems. It is usually the slowest of the transfer protocols, but there may be times when KERMIT is the only protocol that works. The Terminal program, which comes with Windows, offers KERMIT, as do a number of other communications programs.

In truth, KERMIT need not be slow, and some programs that adhere to the KERMIT protocol are quite speedy indeed. However, unless you plan to roam the Net looking for fast KERMIT-compliant file-transfer programs (which you can, of course, do — there are plenty of them on the Net), you are probably stuck with whatever KERMIT program came with your communications software. Unfortunately, there is a good chance that that program will transfer files very slowly. For example, you are likely to grow old waiting for Windows' Terminal program to transfer files using the KERMIT protocol. Unless you have facts to the contrary at your disposal, then, you are probably best off assuming that transferring files using the KERMIT protocol is likely to take a while.

## XMODEM

XMODEM was the first file transfer protocol to become widely known. It was invented by Ward Christiansen, who, not entirely coincidentally, was also the first operator of a BBS (bulletin board system).

The oldest version of XMODEM uses an error-checking method called *checksum*. With this method, the receiving computer sums up the bytes it receives and compares the total with that sent by the sending computer, which has been doing the same thing. This method is not as accurate as error-checking methods developed later, and, as you will see, newer versions of XMODEM have been modified to use other error-checking strategies.

An XMODEM-based file transfer program sends packets of 128 bytes each, one packet at a time. Every time it sends a packet, it waits for the receiving computer to acknowledge receipt of the packet before sending the next one. This makes the transmission process slower than with newer protocols, which send larger packets and may be able to send more than one at a time.

XMODEM is the most commonly used protocol. If your communications software offers only one protocol, chances are it's XMODEM. After KERMIT, XMODEM also tends to be the slowest protocol, and it doesn't have many of the nicer features of some protocols developed later. However, if you are patient, or if you only download the occasional not-too-large file, XMODEM could well be the only protocol you need.

## XMODEM Variants: CRC, 1K and YMODEM

**XMODEM-CRC** signified one of the first big improvements to XMODEM. It uses an error-checking process called *cyclic redundancy checking*, or CRC. This makes XMODEM transmissions more accurate, although no faster, than standard XMODEM. Since being developed, it has been implemented in the majority of programs that adhere to XMODEM's protocol. Programs following the XMODEM-CRC protocol actually have a choice: if the receiving program with which they are communicating can transmit and receive using CRC, both programs do so; otherwise, they automatically switch to traditional checksum error checking.

**XMODEM-1K** introduced an improvement in transfer speed over high-quality telephone lines. It divides the files it transfers into packets of 1024 bytes each; this is in contrast to a packet size of 128 bytes for "plain" XMODEM. XMODEM-1K thus sends more data at a time with fewer stops for acknowledgments from the receiving system. With a phone line of reasonable quality, this leads to a significant increase in speed.

 If you use XMODEM-1K, but find that your transfer speed seems to be slower than with plain XMODEM, chances are you have a noisy phone line. If this is the case, the sending computer is encountering a significant number of errors during the transmission, and it has to keep resending those big packets, thus resulting in a slower transfer rate than with XMODEM.

**YMODEM**, developed by Chuck Forsberg, was another big step forward in the advancement of file transfer protocols. It has all the features of XMODEM-1K, plus it can bundle and send multiple files at one time. It also sends along the creation date and the original name for each file sent.

## ZMODEM

The ZMODEM protocol was also created by Chuck Forsberg, and it's our choice for speed, accuracy, and number of slick features. It is what's known as a *streaming protocol*: it can send packets continuously without waiting for an acknowledgment, and there is no limit to the number of packets it has "in the air," so to speak. ZMODEM also has an autostart feature, which means you don't have to instruct the receiving computer to receive the file; ZMODEM handles that for you. This is very convenient.

ZMODEM can send multiple files in one transfer, can restart a failed transmission at the point where it failed, and is generally the fastest of the protocols, provided your phone line is not too noisy. If you do have a noisy phone line, you may find that a ZMODEM-based file transfer is very slow, because it may have to resend a lot of data when it detects an error in the transfer.

 Not all communications software offers ZMODEM, but if it's available, it's definitely the protocol to try first. If you plan to do a lot of downloading, consider getting a communications program that supports ZMODEM. You won't regret it.

## Summary of Protocols

The following table summarizes the advantages and disadvantages of KERMIT, the XMODEM protocols, and ZMODEM.

### Summary of Protocols

| Protocol | Features/ Advantages | Disadvantages |
|----------|----------------------|---------------|
| KERMIT | Transfers between most systems; works where other protocols fail; MS Terminal supports it. | Often very slow compared with the others. |
| XMODEM | Most PC communications software supports this; uses 128-byte packets. | Slower than most others; transmits only one file at a time; does not send file creation date or time. |

## Summary of Protocols  (Continued)

| Protocol | Features/ Advantages | Disadvantages |
|---|---|---|
| XMODEM-CRC | Better error checking than plain XMODEM; commonly available; MS Terminal supports it. | Same as plain XMODEM. |
| XMODEM-1K | Faster than other versions of XMODEM; uses 1024-byte packets. | Not supported by all communications programs; transmits only one file at a time; does not send file creation date or time. |
| YMODEM | Uses 1024-byte packets; sends multiple files at a time; sends file creation dates and times. | Not supported by all communications programs; usually slower than ZMODEM. |
| ZMODEM | Usually fastest; sends multiple files at a time; sends file creation dates and times; can recover from failed transmissions. | Not all PC communication software supports this; may be slow on noisy phone lines. |

## Choosing a Protocol

With so many protocols available, which do you choose? After all, who knows if you have a noisy phone line? And how noisy is noisy?

We recommend the following strategy. If your communications program supports it, try ZMODEM first. It's usually fastest, and it will work well on most phone lines. If you don't have ZMODEM, try YMODEM or XMODEM-1K. If you get lots of transmission errors using these larger-packet protocols, consider using XMODEM-CRC, plain XMODEM, or KERMIT.

For the empiricists among you, there is another way to find the fastest protocol: try them all. Choose a large file on the Net, then download it once using each protocol available to you. If you really want to get fancy, perform each transfer several times so you can average the results. Then just pick the protocol that gives you the fastest transfer rate.

## Text Files versus Binary Files

In order to successfully download a file, you often need to know whether it's a *text file* or a *binary file*. In general, if you can display the contents of a file on your screen without seeing strange characters or hearing warning beeps, you have a text file in front of you. If not, you have a binary file. Text files often have an extension of *.txt*, but this is not always the case; see Appendix B for a list of other common extensions for text files.

Most downloadable files, however, are binary files. The following are all binary files:

- Executable programs (except *.bat* files)
- Compressed files and file archives
- Files containing images, sounds, and movies

If you're not sure whether a file you want to download is text or binary, assume it's a binary file.

The reason you care whether a file is text or binary is that the programs performing the download need to know. When you initiate a download, you'll often have to specify whether you're downloading a text file or a binary file, and if you happen to get it wrong, the sending and receiving programs won't be able to correct your mistake. Instead, they'll blithely proceed as if you were right, and you'll end up with a new file on your computer that will not behave the way it's supposed to. Then you'll have to download the file again, this time with the correct text-or-binary specification.

## Performing a Download

When you download a file to your computer, you control the whole process. As long as you have a connection to the Net, you don't need anyone at the sending computer to do anything.

There are two steps needed to download a file from the sending computer to your local computer:

1. **Instruct the sending computer to send the file**. Often, you will have to specify whether the file is text or binary.

2. **Instruct your PC to receive the file**, and specify the name of the new file that will be created as a result of the download. If you're using ZMODEM, this step is performed automatically.

How you accomplish these steps depends on the details of the system you've dialed into and on the particular communications software you're running on your PC. In some cases, performing a download is as simple as clicking on a button; everything is handled automatically by the software running on your PC and the computer you've dialed into. More commonly, you'll be presented with a menu of downloading services. In that case, you just need to follow the instructions that go along with the menu.

In some cases, however — especially if you've dialed into a Unix computer (e.g., one that gives you access to the Internet) — you'll need to know the commands to perform the two steps above. We'll show you the most commonly needed commands in a moment.

Of course, if you have a question about downloading in your particular configuration, or if you're not sure exactly how to do things, one way to find out is to experiment. You won't hurt the file or the software if you try to transmit using a method your PC software can't handle. The worst that could happen is a big, fat nothing. Nothing will get transmitted, and the program will end with an error message or sit there until you stop it.

## Downloading Examples

In the examples that follow, we show you exactly how to download both text and binary files. For the purposes of these examples, we assume you dial into a Unix computer and you have to type explicit commands to the Unix computer in order to start a download. We also assume you're using the Windows' Terminal program as your communications software.

You will find that the only difference between the two examples is that in one case you specify you're downloading a text file, while in the other you specify it's a binary file. Everything else is exactly the same, which means it's pretty easy to master the fine art of downloading.

### Downloading a Text File

This is a simple example using XMODEM-CRC as the transfer protocol. MS Terminal supports only XMO-DEM-CRC and KERMIT, but once you understand how to download a file, you can begin to experiment with other communications software and other protocols.

Don't forget, you can even download communications programs from the Net and try them out.

If, in the examples that follow, you have questions about how to use the Terminal program, consult the online help for that program. If you have questions about how to use a Unix system, use the Unix "man" command to consult the online help that Unix makes available.

1. Double-click on the **Accessories** group in the Program Manager, then double-click on the **Terminal** icon to start Terminal. Click on the **Settings** item of the Terminal menu bar, and select **Binary Transfers...**. (In view of the fact that you're going to download a text file, this probably seems like an odd menu choice. All you're doing at this point, however, is specifying the transfer protocol that Terminal should use, and this is the way Terminal lets you do that.) You will be presented with this dialog box:

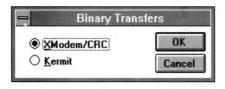

   Click on *XModem/CRC*, then on **OK**. This will establish XMODEM-CRC as the download protocol you wish to use.

2. Dial into your Net computer and find a text file you want to download to your PC. In this example, we assume you want to download a file named *example.txt*.

   Type the following command to the Unix computer:

```
sx -a example.txt
```

This command tells the Unix computer the following:

- The "sx" tells it to start sending a file using the XMODEM protocol.

- The "-a" tells it the file is a text file. (The "a" stands for ASCII, which is a kind of text.)

- The file to be sent is named *example.txt.*

The system responds with a message like this:

```
Sending example.txt, 72 XMODEM
blocks. Give your local XMODEM
receive command now.
```

This message tells you your downloading command has been accepted and the Unix computer is ready to send. Now you must tell your PC to receive the file.

3. Click on the **Transfers** item of the Terminal menu bar. You'll see this pulldown menu:

Select **Receive Binary File...** from this menu. Yes, you're going to be receiving a text file, but you've already told the sending computer that, so you don't need to tell your PC, too. As long as one of the computers knows, the transfer will be handled properly by both sides. Furthermore, if you select **Receive Text File...**, you'll find that the transfer simply doesn't take place.

You'll see a dialog box asking you to specify what name you'd like to give the file you're downloading:

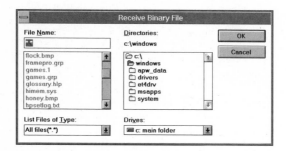

Enter the file name in the box labeled *File Name*. You can enter the same name as on the sending computer (provided it's a legal file name under Windows — not all Unix file names are), or you can enter a different name. In this case, we'll change the name of the file slightly to be *new-text.txt*, and we'll put it into a directory we have reserved for temporary files called *c:\temp*.

To do this, double-click on *c:\* in the *Directories* box. Then double-click on the *temp* directory, and enter newtext.txt in the *File Name* box. The dialog box will look like this:

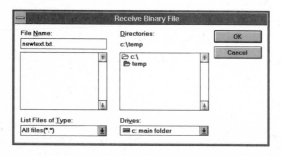

Click on **OK**.

The transmission will now begin. You can monitor the progress of the file transfer by watching Terminal's information bar as it counts the bytes:

| Stop | Bytes: 7040 | Receiving: NEWTEXT.TXT | Retries: 1 |

When the transmission is complete, the information bar will go away, and you will find that you have a new file, *c:\temp\newtext.txt*, on your PC. This file will be identical to the file *example.txt* on the Unix computer from which you downloaded it.

There are two things to observe during the transmission. First, since this download uses XMODEM-CRC, the bytes are counted in increments of 128 — the size of each packet sent. Second, the number of retries shows the number of packets that had to be resent during the download. If there were a lot of retries, your phone line may be comparatively noisy.

## Downloading a Binary File

For this example, we'll again use MS Terminal as the communications software on your PC, and we'll employ XMODEM-CRC as the file transfer protocol.

1.  Do exactly what you did in Step 1 of the text file transfer to specify that you wish to use the XMODEM-CRC transfer protocol.

2.  Dial into your Net computer and find a binary file you want to download to your PC. In this example, we assume you want to download a file named *example.exe*.

    Type the following command to the Unix computer:

    ```
    sx -b example.exe
    ```

    This command tells the Unix computer the following:

    ■ The "sx" tells it to start sending a file using the XMODEM protocol.

- The "-b" tells it the file is a binary file.
- The file to be sent is named *example.exe*.

The system responds with a message like this:

```
Sending example.exe, 1145 XMO-
DEM blocks. Give your local XMO-
DEM receive command now.
```

This message tells you your downloading command has been accepted, and the Unix computer is ready to send. Now you must tell your PC to receive the file.

3.  Do exactly what you did in Step 3 of the text file transfer to specify the name you'd like the file you're downloading to have. The file transfer will proceed exactly as it did in the previous example.

## Using Other Protocols

The two downloading examples both employed the XMODEM-CRC protocol, but what would happen if you had a communications program that allowed you to use other protocols? What if you decided you wanted to use a protocol other than XMODEM-CRC?

Happily, very little would change. In fact, if you decided to use the original XMODEM protocol or the XMODEM-1K protocol, nothing at all would change — you'd follow the steps in the example just as they are.

If you used YMODEM, you'd type "sy" instead of "sx" when you initiated the download in Step 2, and everything else would be the same.

 If you wanted to use ZMODEM, you'd type "sz" instead of "sx" in Step 2, but you wouldn't perform Step 3 at all, because the ZMODEM protocol handles that step automatically. However, when using ZMODEM, the name of the downloaded file automatically becomes the same as the name of the file on the computer you're connected to, so if you wanted to give the downloaded file a different name (as we did in the example), you'd have to use the File Manager to rename the downloaded file after the download was complete.

Finally, if you used KERMIT, things would be a bit different. For the text file transfer, you'd type this command to the Unix computer in Step 2 (instead of the "sx" command):

```
kermit -s example.txt
```

For the binary file transfer, you'd type this:

```
kermit -i -s example.exe
```

As we said before, however, we suggest you turn to KERMIT only as a last resort.

## Downloading Tips

Choosing a transfer protocol is one of the most important decisions you must make when you download, but there is more to successful downloading than just deciding what protocol to use. In the remainder of this chapter, we discuss how to configure your phone line so you won't be interrupted when downloading, how to avoid downloading outdated versions of programs, how to prevent your PC from becoming infected by computer viruses, and how to tell the File Manager about new types of files you've downloaded.

## Configuring Your Phone Line

If you are using a telephone line that has call waiting or some other service that could interrupt the line while you're connected, turn it off before dialing into the Net.

Your telephone company is almost certainly able to provide you with a numeric sequence you can punch in to your telephone to turn call waiting off and on. Use it. With call waiting on, the beeping sound caused by an incoming call can be interpreted as bad data by your PC or by the computer you're communicating with. This can slow down a file transfer significantly, because it will usually result in the transferring program having to resend a large number of packets. In extreme cases, it can cause your connection to the Net to be terminated. Either way, it will cause major and unnecessary headaches.

Once you've disconnected from the Net and hung up the phone, of course, you should be sure to punch in the magic sequence of numbers that will reactivate call waiting (or whatever service you use).

In a similar vein, each time you prepare to dial out to the Net, get into the habit of warning other members of your household who may want to use the same phone line. If they try to use the telephone while you're downloading, they're going to get an earful of unpleasant modem sounds, and your download is likely to be slowed down or prematurely terminated.

## Identifying Program Versions

Computer programs are identified in terms of their *version numbers*, with higher numbers identifying more recent (and presumably better) versions of programs. For example, Windows version 3.1 is more recent (and presumably better) than Windows version 3.0.

Programs on the Net, too, use version numbers, and often the version number of a program is incorporated into the name of the file containing the program. If, for example, you see a file on the Net called *lha213.exe*, that means you've found a program called LHA, version 2.13. (LHA is an archiving and compression program and is included as part of this book. You will read all about LHA in Chapter 4.) Similarly, if you encounter a file named *wplny09c.zip*, that means you've found version 0.9c of WPLAny, a sound-playing program. (WPLAny is also included with this book, and you'll learn how to use it in Chapter 6.)

 Higher version numbers tend to indicate later, more mature, versions of programs than lower numbers. Version numbers less than 1.0 (such as WPLAny's 0.9c) generally correspond to programs that are still somewhat under development. Such programs may be less stable or may not be as fully featured as programs placed on the Net with versions numbered 1.0 or higher.

The Net has a long memory, and it's a simple fact that there are file archives on the Net that haven't been updated in years. This can create some problems when you're looking for a particular file or program. For instance, you may be looking for a shareware program, but unless you know the specific version of the program you want to download, you might wind up downloading an outdated version. This is not an uncommon problem: when last we checked, there were a good half-dozen versions of an unarchiving program called ARCE available on the Net. Some were over six years old!

In order to make sure you're getting the latest (and presumably greatest) version of a program, try to perform a search for all versions of the program that are available. Then download the one with the highest version number.

Another approach is to check the creation dates of the files you are interested in downloading, because files created more recently are usually more up-to-date than older files. You have to be careful when going by creation dates, however, because sometimes the creation date you'll see is the date when the *copy* of the file you're looking at was created, not when the information inside the file was created. For this reason, version numbers are generally more reliable.

## Avoiding Computer Viruses

 Any time you download files from another computer system to your PC, you have to worry about the problem of introducing a computer virus. Such viruses may cause serious problems (including loss of data) and can be very difficult to remove from your computer.

On the one hand, viruses are less likely to be found in software downloaded from the Net than you might fear. System operators (SysOps) are generally on the lookout for them, and many SysOps — especially those on BBS systems and on commercial services like CompuServe and America Online — pride themselves on maintaining virus-free download areas. On the other hand, some SysOps are less vigilant than others, so viruses may fall through the cracks on some systems.

And then there's the matter of the Internet, a system that not only has no real SysOp, it's so big and is growing so fast that no SysOp could realistically check each of its millions of downloadable files to ensure that they contain no known viruses. Viruses are therefore a problem that cannot be realistically ignored.

Computer viruses are usually located in an executable file, such as one ending in *.exe*, *.com*, or *.bat*. Viruses are activated when you execute the file they're hiding in, so the best time to check for viruses in downloaded programs is *before* you run the programs. That's the purpose of virus-detection programs: to examine other files to see if any known viruses are hiding inside them.

Virus-detection programs can detect many viruses, but none can guarantee it will catch all possible viruses. New virus strains are regularly created by unscrupulous programmers, so the viruses recognized today will be only some of the viruses that will be recognized tomorrow. For that reason, it's a good idea to update your virus-detection program periodically. One of the books we recommend, Bernard Aboba's *Online User's Encyclope-*

*dia* (see Chapter 7), contains a list of recommended virus-detection programs, both shareware and commercial, and we suggest you look this list over.

This is not something to panic over, though. The evildoers who write viruses and other intentionally destructive programs are a small minority of the hacker population, and the vast majority of software available on the Net is virus-free. As long as you are fairly diligent about checking new executable files for viruses, you will most likely have no trouble.

One of the programs included with this book, WinZip, can automatically check for viruses in the files you download, and it understands how to use the most common virus-detection programs available. WinZip's ability to automatically check files for viruses is one of many reasons why we believe you'll come to view it as an indispensable part of your downloading toolbox. WinZip is described in detail in Chapter 4.

## Modifying File Manager Associations

When you double-click on a file in the File Manager, the File Manager tries to automatically start up the program that is appropriate for the contents of that file. For example, if you double-click on a text file, the File Manager will run Notepad to let you view or edit the contents of the file.

The File Manager knows what program to run for a particular file by looking at the file's extension. Each extension the File Manager knows about is *associated* with a particular program. For example, the extension *.txt* is associated with the program *notepad.exe*, and that's how the File Manager knows it should run Notepad when you double-click on text files.

 You can change the associations used by the File Manager. For example, if you have a different text-editing program you'd prefer to use for text files (instead of Notepad), you can follow the instructions below to change the association for

*.txt* files to the name of your preferred program. The Net offers a number of text-editing programs, and if you're dissatisfied with Notepad, we encourage you to download a more powerful text editor.

Possibly even more useful than changing File Manager associations, however, is adding new ones. Suppose, for example, you start downloading *.voc* files, which, as we explain in Chapter 6, contain sounds. You're likely to want to associate *.voc* files with the program *wplany.exe*, because you have that program available (it comes with this book), and it knows how to play *.voc* files through your PC's sound card. This is how you'd associate *wplany.exe* with *.voc* files:

1. Select the **Associate...** item from the File Manager's **File** menu. You will see the Associate dialog box:

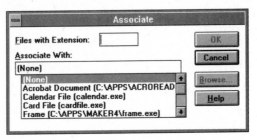

2. In the *Files with Extension* box, enter "VOC".

3. In the *Associate With* box, enter the full path-name of the *wplany.exe* program. If you installed the software according to the installation summary at the end of Chapter 1, you'd enter "c:\wplany\wplany.exe".

4. Click on **OK**.

That's all there is to it. From this point forward, any time you double-click on a file with the *.voc* extension, the File Manager will automatically run *wplany.exe* to play the sound in the file you double-clicked.

For more information about setting up file associations in the File Manager, consult the File Manager's online help; search for help on "associating files."

# File Compression and File Archives

In Chapter 1, we mentioned that downloadable files on the Net are often compressed to save disk space. We also pointed out that files related to one another (such as programs and their associated documentation) are usually bundled together into special types of files called *archives*. In this chapter, we explain file compression and file archives in greater detail. We also introduce WinZip, a program included with this book that allows you to manipulate compressed files and file archives with the same ease with which you currently manipulate your disk files using the File Manager.

## Compressing and Archiving Files

To *compress* a file is to reduce the size of that file, typically without losing any of the information inside it (see Figure 4). There are a number of different techniques for compressing files, and different techniques generally produce different degrees of compression. Some techniques achieve better degrees of compression on certain types of files than on others. Unfortunately, there is no single technique that achieves the best degree of compression for all files. For example, in Chapter 6 we'll examine a technique called JPEG compression, which yields dramatic results when put to work on files containing pictures, but doesn't work at all for files containing programs.

*Compressing a File*

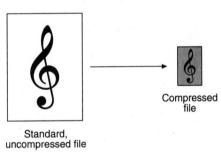

Compressed
file

Standard,
uncompressed file

Figure 4

*Archiving* is the process of bundling a set of files together into one file (see Figure 5). Generally, a file archive will contain a group of related files. For example, an archive may contain an executable program, which is one file, and its associated documentation, which is a separate file.

*Archiving Files*

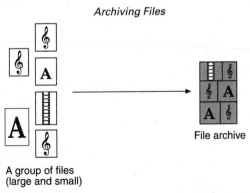

File archive

A group of files
(large and small)

Figure 5

One of the most common reasons for creating file archives (and the one of primary interest to you as a downloader) is that they are convenient for moving files between computers. It's certainly a lot easier to download one archive containing 200 files than to download those 200 files one by one.

Still, a file archive containing 200 files is usually too big to comfortably handle. It takes up at least as much disk space as the 200 files inside it, and 200 files can take up a lot of disk space. As fate would have it, however, most archiving programs also perform file compression, so in practice, you both compress and archive a group of files in a single step (see Figure 6).

*Compressing and Archiving Files*

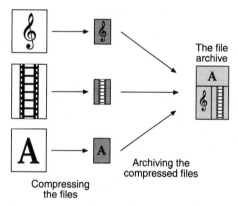

Figure 6

Almost all files on the Net that are designed to be downloaded are in the form of archives containing one or more compressed files. If you want to become proficient at downloading, then, it is important that you become adept at recognizing such archives and at working with them. Fortunately, this is not difficult to do.

## Identifying Archive Types

Files on the Net are named in such a way as to let you know which, if any, of the many archiving and compression techniques was employed to create them. In particular, the *extension* of a file's name tells you if it's an archive and, if so, which technique was used to generate the archive.

There are a number of different archiving techniques, hence a number of different file extensions for archives (see Appendix B), but the most important archive extension for PC and Windows users is *.zip*. A file with a name ending in *.zip* is an archive that was created using the PKZip technique. You will quickly become familiar with *ZIP files*, as they are called, because the vast majority of files on the Net that are designed to be downloaded to PCs are ZIP files.

There are other file extensions that identify archives, of course, extensions like *.lzh*, *.arj*, *.arc*, and *.zoo*, but it's not necessary to commit such alphabet soup to memory. When you encounter a file extension on the Net you don't recognize, just consult Appendix A. It'll quickly tell you whether the extension indicates an archive, and, if it does, it'll tell you what program you should use to access the files in the archive. If the extension doesn't correspond to an archive, it'll tell you that, too, and it'll also tell you what the file probably *does* contain.

What it all boils down to is simple. ZIP file archives end in *.zip*, and you need to remember that. Other archive formats use different file extensions, but you don't need to remember those extensions, because you can look them up in Appendices A and B whenever you need to.

## Uncompressing and Unarchiving Files

Once you download an archive, what do you do with it? After all, the files within the archive are useless to you until they've been *extracted* (copied out of the archive) and uncompressed.

Fortunately, many programs know how to perform such extraction and uncompression. Usually, if a program knows how to create a particular kind of archive (a ZIP file, say), it also knows how to extract and uncompress files that are in that kind of archive. So if you download a particular kind of archive, all you need is a program that understands that type of archive. If you don't have such a program installed on your machine, of course, you can always download one from the Net.

But that leads to a new problem. If you need software from the Net in order to work with file archives, and if most software on the Net is stored in the form of file archives, how do you open the archives that contain the programs you need to open the archives?

## Self-Extracting Archives

Some programs — especially programs that create and manipulate file archives — are stored on the Net in a format known as a *self-extracting archive* (SEA). An SEA is a file that is both an executable program *and* an archive. Once you have downloaded an SEA to your PC, all you need to do is run it in the same way you'd run any other program. For example, you can double-click on it in the File Manager.

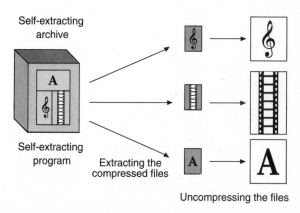

Self-extracting archive

Self-extracting program

Extracting the compressed files

Uncompressing the files

Figure 7

When an SEA is executed, it automatically extracts and uncompresses the files contained within it. When it's done, you're left with the original SEA, plus uncompressed copies of all the files it contains (see Figure 7).

SEAs are a clever solution to the how-do-I-unarchive-the-unarchiving-software problem, but they do have one drawback: it's difficult to distinguish them from conventional executable programs. After all, both SEAs and conventional programs have the same *.exe* file extension. How, then, do you distinguish one from the other? Unfortunately, there's no reliable way to tell. If you see a file on the Net with a *.exe* extension, about the only way to find out if it's an SEA is to download the file and give it a test drive.

SEAs are almost always DOS programs (as opposed to Windows programs), but you can run them under Windows anyway. When you do, don't be alarmed when Windows briefly goes away and displays a DOS prompt. When Windows returns, the SEA will have completed its task, and the files in the archive will have been extracted. If you don't like the startling change to your screen that occurs when you run an SEA from Windows, you might consider running it from a DOS window instead. Either way, you'll end up with the same files being extracted from the SEA.

## *Using WinZip to Work with Archives*

If all the archives on the Net were stored as SEAs, there'd be no need to learn how to work with them directly. Most Net archives, however, are not in the form of SEAs, so you do need to learn how to manipulate them. For that purpose, Nico Mak's shareware program, WinZip, is the downloader's gift from heaven.

We really can't say enough about this program. WinZip gives you a nice graphical interface that lets you manipulate file archives in just about any way it makes sense for file archives to be manipulated. Furthermore, WinZip does this for more than just ZIP files. It also understands archives in the LZH, ARJ, and ARC formats; we'll have more to say about these formats shortly. These four archive formats together account for almost every archive you're ever likely to download, so WinZip is probably the only archive-manipulation program you'll ever need to learn how to use.

Perhaps most important, WinZip is easy to use. This program can dramatically ease the stress and frustration that can come from working with compressed and archived files. With WinZip, downloading for Windows is, well, a zip!

## An Overview of WinZip

When you open an archive for viewing in WinZip, you'll see a window similar to this one:

| Name | Date | Time | Size | Ratio | Packed | Path |
|------|------|------|------|-------|--------|------|
| commdlg.dll | 10/04/92 | 19:30 | 89,248 | 50% | 44,632 | |
| ebdcntrl.dll | 10/04/92 | 19:30 | 62,976 | 67% | 21,138 | |
| grabpro.doc | 10/04/92 | 20:00 | 25,873 | 68% | 8,536 | |
| grabpro.exe | 10/04/92 | 19:30 | 89,088 | 59% | 36,543 | |
| grabpro.hlp | 10/04/92 | 19:30 | 43,566 | 19% | 35,332 | |
| readme.txt | 10/04/92 | 19:30 | 224 | 41% | 133 | |
| register.frm | 10/04/92 | 19:30 | 3,895 | 58% | 1,654 | |
| register.txt | 10/04/92 | 19:30 | 2,162 | 45% | 1,192 | |
| vendor.txt | 10/04/92 | 19:59 | 2,486 | 49% | 1,275 | |

Selected 0 files, 0 bytes    Total 9 files, 313KB

For each file in the archive, WinZip provides the following information:

- The **name** of the file.

- The **date** and **time** of the most recent change to the file.

- The original (uncompressed) **size** of the file (in bytes).

- The compression **ratio** achieved for the file. A ratio of 50% means the compressed version of the file is half as big as the original. A ratio of 67% means the compressed version of the file is about a third of the size of the original file, and so on.

- The compressed ("**packed**") size of the file (in bytes).

- The **path** leading to the file. This is usually blank, but if an archive contains files that were originally in a number of different directories, the path will specify the directory in which the file was found. WinZip can use this information to ensure that files are placed in the proper location when they are extracted. This capability allows WinZip to recreate entire DOS directory structures that have been archived.

Simple commands in WinZip let you view, virus-check, extract, and run files in an archive. Other commands allow you to add files to and remove files from an archive. You can even test an archive to see if it's become corrupted (which is possible when downloading over a noisy phone line). All these capabilities are available to you through a simple point-and-click interface that's as easy to use as the File Manager.

Finally, WinZip helps you make good use of your precious disk space. With WinZip, you can view the contents of an archive, and you can even run the programs and view the documents within, all without permanently extracting and uncompressing any files that would take up space on your disk.

## Installing WinZip

Installing WinZip is straightforward, but because WinZip can do so much for you, you need to take a little time to configure it properly. Everything you need to do is described below, so just take it step by step, and you'll have WinZip installed before you know it.

1. **Create directory and copy WinZip from the diskette**: Create a new directory on your hard drive for WinZip. You can use whatever directory you like, but we recommend you use *c:\winzip*, and in the instructions that follow, we assume that's the directory you'll use.

   Copy the self-extracting archive *winzip5b.exe* from the *programs* directory of this book's diskette into *c:\winzip*.

2. **Extract files**: In the File Manager, double-click on *c:\winzip\winzip5b.exe*. In moments, the files contained inside the archive will be installed on your hard disk. Press F5 to make the File Manager update itself and show you these new files.

3. **Start WinZip**: In the File Manager, double-click on *c:\winzip\winzip.exe*; this will start WinZip. A window will come up summarizing the features of the program. Click on **OK**. Then you'll be presented with a dialog box that contains information about WinZip's licensing agreement. To continue, you'll have to click on **I Agree**.

4. **Specify a virus-detection program**: You'll then see a dialog box that looks like this:

```
┌──────────────────────────────────────────────────────┐
│ ▬          WinZip Program Locations                    │
├──────────────────────────────────────────────────────┤
│ Some optional WinZip features require external programs. ┌─────────┐ │
│ If you are not familiar with these programs just press OK. │   OK    │ │
│ Leave fields empty if programs are not installed.         └─────────┘ │
│                                                      ┌─────────┐ │
│ For help press the F1 key or push the Help button.   │ Cancel  │ │
│                                                      └─────────┘ │
│                                                      ┌─────────┐ │
│                                                      │  Help   │ │
│                                                      └─────────┘ │
│                                                                  │
│   PKZIP:          [                              ]               │
│   PKUNZIP:        [                              ]               │
│   ZIP2EXE:        [                              ]               │
│   ARJ             [                              ]               │
│   LHA:            [                              ]               │
│   ARC Extraction: [                            ] [±]             │
│   Default Association: [C:\WINDOWS\NOTEPAD.EXE  ]               │
│                                                                  │
│  ┌─ Virus Scanner ────────────────────────────────────────────┐ │
│  │ Scan Program:   [                          ] [±]            │ │
│  │ Parameters:     [                            ]              │ │
│  │        ☐ Run In Iconized DOS Session If Possible           │ │
│  └────────────────────────────────────────────────────────────┘ │
│                                                                  │
│ Directories specified by the PATH= environment variable          │
│ are searched if a directory is not specified                     │
└──────────────────────────────────────────────────────┘
```

 You can ignore most of this box for now, but if you have a virus-detection program on your PC and you'd like WinZip to run it for you automatically when you install newly-downloaded software (which we recommend), you need to tell WinZip about your virus-detection program. Now is the time to do it.

The bottom part of the dialog box contains fields for you to enter information about your virus-detection program (which WinZip calls a *virus scanner*):

```
┌─ Virus Scanner ───────────────────────────────────────┐
│ Scan Program:   [                              ] [±]   │
│ Parameters:     [                              ]       │
│        ☐ Run In Iconized DOS Session If Possible       │
└────────────────────────────────────────────────────────┘
```

In the *Scan Program* box, enter the DOS command that's used to run your virus scanner. Even if you haven't explicitly installed a special virus-detection program, you may still have one on your computer, because many recent versions of DOS come with a virus-scanning program as standard equipment. Versions 6.0 and higher of MS-DOS, for example, come with the MSAV (*Microsoft Anti-Virus*) program.

 If you're not sure if you have a virus-detection program, click the down-pointing arrow opposite the *Scan Program* box for a list of programs WinZip knows about. (MSAV is on this list.) If you don't recognize any of the programs, you can use trial and error to see if any of them is installed on your machine. Just click on one, say MSAV.EXE, then click the dialog box's **OK** button. If this program is *not* installed on your DOS path, WinZip will alert you with this message:

When you click **OK** to acknowledge this message, you'll be returned to the previous dialog box, and you can try another program in the list. If WinZip does not issue an alert message like the one above, it means the virus-detection program you selected *is* installed on your machine, and WinZip will use that virus-detection program in the future.

Once you've specified the virus-checking program, you will also have to fill in the *Parameters* box so WinZip knows what parameters to pass to your virus scanner each time WinZip runs it. If your virus scanner is one WinZip knows about, WinZip itself fills in the parameters. For example,

if you choose MSAV from the pulldown list, Win-
Zip fills in the parameters as shown below:

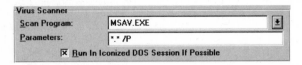

If you don't have one of the virus-detection programs WinZip is aware of, you'll have to consult
the documentation for your virus-detection program to find out what parameters should be
passed to that program when WinZip runs it. You
can also click on the dialog box's **Help** button to
read WinZip's online documentation about how
to fill in the fields of the *Virus Scanner* part of
the dialog box.

If you have no virus-detection program, leave
the fields blank, and make a note to yourself to
consider getting such a program in the future.
When you do, you can go back and tell WinZip
about it.

When you're done filling in the dialog box, click
**OK**.

5.  **Choose whether to add WinZip to the
    Accessories group**: You'll be asked if you'd
    like a WinZip icon to be added to the Accesso-
    ries group of the Program Manager. Answer the
    question according to your preference: **Yes** if
    you'd like a WinZip icon to be added, **No** other-
    wise. We recommend you click on **Yes** to add
    the icon, because then you'll be able to start
    WinZip by simply double-clicking on its icon in
    the Program Manager.

6.  **Choose whether to set up File Manager
    associations**: Depending on how your PC is
    configured, you may see the following dialog
    box:

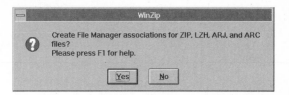

If you are presented with this box, click on **Yes** if
you wish to have the File Manager automatically
use WinZip to manipulate archives in the ZIP,
LZH, ARJ, and ARC formats. We strongly recommend you click on **Yes**. If you are not presented with this box, WinZip will set up these
associations automatically.

7. **Specify an extraction directory**: You will now
   see the main WinZip window. Click on the
   **Options** menu, then select **Directories...**. You
   will be presented with this dialog box:

You can ignore most of this box, but be sure that in the *Default Extract Directory* section, "Open Archive Directory" is selected, like this:

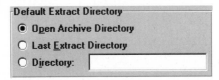

If it's not selected, click on it. Then click on **OK** to close the dialog box. That will return you to the main WinZip window, and you should then exit the program by choosing **Exit** from the **File** menu.

8.  **Delete unnecessary file**: You no longer need the file *winzip5b.exe* that's in your *c:\winzip* directory; it's just a copy of the same file that's in the *programs* directory of this book's diskette. We recommend you conserve space on your hard disk by deleting *c:\winzip\winzip5b.exe*.

Congratulations! You've just given birth to a bouncing baby program: WinZip is now installed.

## WinZip Commands

As is the case with many Windows programs, there are several ways to issue commands in WinZip. Learning your way around WinZip is fun, and we take fun very seriously in this book. Here's a list of the most useful WinZip commands, as well as the buttons and menu choices that let you issue them.

### WinZip Commands

| Button | Menu Sequence | What It Does |
|--------|---------------|-------------|
| New | FILE ↓ NEW ARCHIVE | Creates a new archive so you can add files to it. |

## WinZip Commands (Continued)

| Button | Menu Sequence | What It Does |
|--------|---------------|--------------|
| Open | FILE ↓ OPEN ARCHIVE | Examines the contents of an existing archive. You can then view, run, and extract the files in the archive. |
| Add | ACTIONS ↓ ADD | Adds one or more files to an archive. This could be a new archive or one that's been opened. |
| Extract | ACTIONS ↓ EXTRACT | Extracts some or all of the files in an archive and write them to disk. |
| View | ACTIONS ↓ VIEW | Views the contents of a text file that's contained in an archive. |
| CheckOut | ACTIONS ↓ CHECKOUT | Tentatively extracts the files stored in an archive and creates a Program Manager group containing icons for the archive's files. |

## Using WinZip

WinZip is such a useful program, we're going to walk you through a complete example of its use in examining an archive, evaluating the contents of that archive, and ultimately, installing the contents of the archive to disk. The example that follows is typical of the way in which you're likely to use WinZip every day.

The most common way to acquire a file archive is by downloading it from the Net, but the following example uses an archive we've provided with this book, one called *odometer.zip*. You'll find it in the *samples* directory of this book's diskette.

The archive *odometer.zip* contains a cute, though silly, freeware program called **Odometer**. It was written by Dean Thomas. Odometer keeps track of the distance your mouse travels. Not only does it tally up the accumulated miles, you can choose to view the distance in kilometers, meters, feet, centimeters, or inches. It's fun, and you'll be surprised at how far your mouse goes in a session.

 Before you can run through this example, you need to have installed WinZip. If you haven't, follow the instructions beginning on page 53. Then follow the steps below to evaluate and install Odometer.

1. **Create a directory for temporary files**: You will need a directory on your hard disk where you can store temporary files. We assume you'll use *c:\temp*, and you should create this directory if it does not already exist. Of course, you are free to use any directory you like for temporary files, but in the instructions that follow, we assume you'll use *c:\temp*.

2. **Copy the Odometer archive**: Copy *odometer.zip* from the *samples* directory of the book's diskette to *c:\temp*.

3. **Launch WinZip**: From the File Manager, double-click on the copy of *odometer.zip* in *c:\temp*; this will start WinZip. After you acknowledge that you are running an unregistered copy of WinZip, you will be presented with the main WinZip window, which shows you the files making up the Odometer archive:

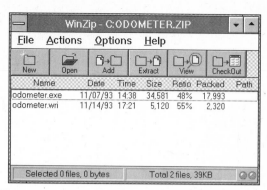

There are only two files in this archive, an execut-able file (*odometer.exe*) and a document pre-pared by Microsoft Write (*odometer.wri*). Many shareware authors use Write files for their docu-mentation, because they know that everybody has Write: it comes as a standard application with Windows.

4. **Make a tentative installation**: Downloading files from the Net is a bit like fishing, because you're never quite sure in advance if what you're reeling in is worth keeping. As a result, the first thing you usually want to do with a newly down-loaded archive is *check it out*: take a quick look at it before determining whether you want to keep it. WinZip understands this well, and all you need to do to check out an archive is click on WinZip's **CheckOut** button. When you do this for *odometer.zip*, you'll see this dialog box:

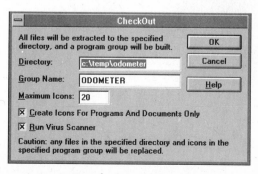

Unless you tell it otherwise, WinZip will create a new temporary directory into which to extract the contents of the archive. In this case, it will use c:\temp\odometer. It will also create a new temporary, Program Manager group called ODOMETER, which will contain icons for files in the archive.

There are two check-boxes at the bottom of the dialog box, and you will usually want to check them both. The *Create Icons For Programs And Documents Only* box controls whether WinZip generates Program Manager icons for every file in the archive or only for the files that are programs or documents. In the case of Odometer, this setting won't make any difference (each of the two files is either a program or a document), but many archives contain lots of files that are neither programs nor documents, and having icons for them does little more than clutter up the Program Manager.

The *Run Virus Scanner* box controls whether WinZip automatically subjects each file in the archive to inspection by your virus-detection program. Unless you like to live dangerously, having WinZip perform such a scan is almost always a good idea. In this particular case, there is no need to scan the archive's files for viruses, because every file on *The Downloader's Companion*'s diskette was checked for viruses before it was approved for shipment with the book. In general, however, you should always subject new programs to a virus-checker's scrutiny, and that's what's shown in this example.

When you are satisfied with the settings in the dialog box, click OK. WinZip will extract each file in the archive into the specified directory and will check each for viruses. When it's done, a new Program Manager group will be created. It will look like this:

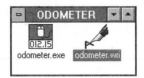

5. **Experiment with Odometer**: You can treat these new Program Manager icons like all other Program Manager icons. Double-click on the *odometer.wri* icon to see the documentation for Odometer. Double-click on the *odometer.exe* icon to run the program. After moving your mouse around a bit and changing the units to kilometers, your odometer might look like this:

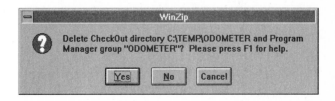

Play around with the program some more, explore its options, and see if you like it. Decide whether you want to install Odometer more permanently or remove it from your PC.

6. **Remove the tentative installation**: When you've reached a decision, exit the Odometer program and select **Close Archive** from Win-Zip's **File** menu. You'll see the following box:

---
**WinZip**

❓ Delete CheckOut directory C:\TEMP\ODOMETER and Program Manager group "ODOMETER"? Please press F1 for help.

[ Yes ]    [ No ]    [ Cancel ]
---

Click on **Yes**. If you're still running Odometer, you'll get all kinds of error messages, because WinZip is unable to remove a tentative installation when files which are part of that installation are still in use. So be sure to shut down

Odometer before you try to close the archive containing it.

When WinZip closes the archive, it also removes the tentative installation, including the files it copied to disk, the directory it created, and the group and icons it added to the Program Manager. This is the beauty of WinZip's **CheckOut** feature: if you decide you don't want to keep a program you've downloaded, WinZip automatically performs the necessary cleanup operations.

If you decided not to keep Odometer, you'd exit WinZip here and be done. For the purposes of this example, we assume you like Odometer well enough to keep it.

7. **Open the archive again**: Click on WinZip's **Open** button, and use the resulting dialog box to tell WinZip to open *c:\temp\odometer.zip* again:

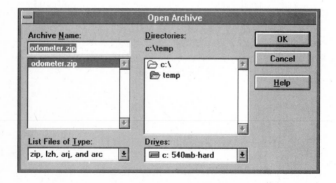

8. **Make a permanent installation**: Click on **CheckOut** again, but this time specify a different directory, one where you'd like the files to permanently reside. A likely location would be *c:\odometer*, in which case the dialog box would look like this:

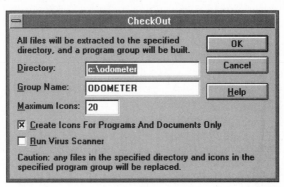

Because you already checked the archive's files for viruses when you made the tentative installation, there is no point in doing it again; that's why *Run Virus Scanner* isn't checked.

Click the **OK** button, and seconds later, the *odometer.exe* and *odometer.wri* files will show up in the *c:\odometer* directory, and a new Program Manager group will be created for Odometer.

9.  **Exit WinZip**: The files in the archive have now been installed, so exit WinZip, then click on **No** when the following question appears:

The installation of odometer is now complete.

In the last step of this example, you specified *c:\odometer* as the directory into which the files in *odometer.zip* should be extracted. If this directory did not exist at the time you performed the extraction, WinZip created it automatically. Having WinZip automatically create new directories for you can be convenient, but it's a double-edged sword.

When specifying the directory into which you want an archive to be extracted, be sure you specify the correct directory, because if you make a mistake, WinZip won't give you a chance to confirm that you want it to create a new directory. Of course, if WinZip creates a directory you don't want, you can always delete the directory and perform the CheckOut again, this time being careful to specify the correct directory name.

## Running Programs from WinZip

The main WinZip window behaves a lot like the File Manager, because you can double-click on files listed in a WinZip window, and the appropriate program will automatically be launched for that type of file. For example, if a file ends in *.exe*, *.com*, *.bat,* or *.pif,* WinZip will execute that file as a program. For other file extensions, WinZip consults the File Manager's list of associations to determine which program to run.

What this means is that you can manipulate the contents of an archive as though the files in that archive were on your hard disk. However, the files themselves remain compressed and bundled inside the archive. If you double-click on a file in an archive, WinZip will, if necessary, temporarily extract and uncompress that file so it can be used by the program with which it is associated, but when that program finishes, WinZip will remove the temporary file from your hard drive. WinZip therefore allows you to manipulate files inside archives as conveniently as the File Manager lets you manipulate files on your PC's disks.

## For More Information

There's more to WinZip than we've described — much more. We encourage you to consult WinZip's extensive online help system, which is available to you, naturally enough, through the **Help**

item on WinZip's menu bar. Pull down the **Help** menu to see a list of general topics, and start exploring from there. Alternatively, you can double-click on *c:\winzip\winzip.hlp* in the File Manager. That will let you read WinZip's online help without actually running WinZip itself.

You can also find useful information in the *.txt* files that come as part of the WinZip distribution. The file *winzip.txt*, for instance, provides a rather breathless overview of the program's capabilities, plus snippets of rave reviews from various technical publications.

## Registering WinZip

The WinZip agreement states that you have a 21-day trial period to play with the unregistered version of the program, and then it's time to make the big decision: buy or die? In other words, register it or delete it? Although registering the shareware you keep is always the honorable (and legally required) thing to do, registering WinZip gives you some additional benefits. For one thing, the registered version of the program doesn't put up the nagging window reminding you about registering. For another, registered users are entitled to priority treatment when they ask for technical support.

The files *license.txt* and *order.txt* will give you all the information you need to register. At $29, it's the downloader's deal of the century.

## Using WinZip with Other Archiving Programs

Most of the archives you'll download from the Net will be in the form of ZIP files, but many other archive formats exist (see Appendix B), and occasionally you'll download a file in one of these alternative formats.

When you do, you'll want to extract and uncompress the files in the archive. Once you've learned how to use WinZip, however, you won't want to learn how to use a different program to do it.

Fortunately, there's a good chance you won't have to. WinZip knows how to handle more than just ZIP files; it can also work with archives in the ARJ, LZH, and ARC formats. Such archive files have the extensions *.arj*, *.lzh*, and *.arc*, respectively, but you don't have to remember this, because (provided you followed our advice when installing WinZip) you've already set up File Manager associations between these extensions and WinZip (see Step 6 on page 56). Working with these other archive types, then, is as easy as working with ZIP archives: just double-click on the archive in the File Manager, then give the usual WinZip commands.

There is, however, one difference in the way WinZip treats ZIP archives and the way it treats files in the other three formats. When you ask WinZip to do something to a ZIP archive (such as extract and uncompress one or more files), WinZip carries out that action itself. When you ask WinZip to perform the same action on an LZH, ARJ, or ARC archive, WinZip hands the request off to a *separate DOS program*, one that knows how to work with archives of that type. The DOS program is the one that actually carries out the work.

This handing off is invisible to you, and you don't really need to be aware of it, but you have to do two things before it will work. First, for each of the LZH, ARJ, and ARC archive formats, you have to acquire a program that knows how to work with archives in that format. Such programs are widely available on the Net, so downloading one is not difficult, but we have saved you most of the trouble by including two of them with this book. The second thing you have to do is tell WinZip where these programs are located on your disk. Fortunately, it's easy to carry out these steps, and in the sections that follow, we tell you exactly what to do.

## ZIP Files

The program that catapulted ZIP files to the forefront of PC archiving is a shareware program called PKZip. Even now, though Windows programs like WinZip can produce ZIP archives as well as extract files from them, most ZIP files are still produced by PKZip. PKZip is the product of a company called PKWARE, Inc.

There are, in fact, things that PKZip and its companion programs can do that WinZip cannot. You won't need to do these things very often (they include the ability to repair damaged archives and the ability to create an archive that spans multiple floppy disks), but in recognition of the fact that PKZip is the *definitive* program for working with ZIP files, WinZip allows itself to be configured so that commands that affect ZIP files are sent straight to PKZip and are not handled by WinZip itself.

WinZip alone suffices for most downloaders, but if you wish to configure WinZip so that it uses PKZip, you must go to the Net and download the current version of PKZip. As we write this, the current version is 2.04g, but this may have changed by the time you read this book; see the discussion beginning on page 40 for suggestions on how to find the current version of a program on the Net.

If you do not plan to configure WinZip to use PKZip, you can skip the remainder of this section and move on to the discussion of LZH files on page 72. Otherwise, read on for instructions on how to install PKZip and configure WinZip to use it. Remember that PKZip is shareware, so even if you only use it indirectly through WinZip, you are still responsible for registering your copy of the program.

PKZip is distributed as a self-extracting archive, and for the purposes of the installation instructions that follow, we assume the name of the SEA is *pkz204g.exe*. (This is the name of the SEA for PKZip 2.04g.) If you have downloaded a more recent version of PKZip, of course, the SEA will have a different name. For details, refer to the discussion beginning on page 40 that explains how files on the Net are typically named.

To install PKZip and configure WinZip to use it, all you need to do is this:

1. **Create a directory and move PKZip into it**: Create a new directory on your hard drive for PKZip. We recommend you use *c:\pkzip*, and in the instructions that follow, we assume that's the directory you'll use. Move *pkz204g.exe* into *c:\pkzip*.

2. **Extract files**: In the File Manager, double-click on *c:\pkzip\pkz204g.exe*. The files contained inside the SEA will be extracted onto your hard disk. Press F5 to make the File Manager update itself and show you these new files.

3. **Tell WinZip about PKZip**: Start WinZip by double-clicking on its icon in the Program Manager or by double-clicking on *c:\winzip\winzip.exe* in the File Manager. After you acknowledge WinZip's licensing agreement, you'll see WinZip's main window.

   Click on WinZip's **Options** menu, then select **Program Locations...**, and you'll be presented with WinZip's Program Locations dialog box. Fill in the boxes for *PKZIP*, *PKUNZIP*, and *ZIP2EXE* like this:

| | |
|---|---|
| PK**Z**IP: | C:\PKZIP\PKZIP.EXE |
| PK**U**NZIP: | C:\PKZIP\PKUNZIP.EXE |
| ZIP**2**EXE: | C:\PKZIP\ZIP2EXE.EXE |
| **A**RJ | |
| **L**HA: | |
| AR**C** Extraction: | |
| **D**efault Association: | C:\WINDOWS\NOTEPAD.EXE |

Click on **OK** to close the dialog box, then exit WinZip.

That's all you have to do. In the future, whenever you need to work with ZIP files, you can just launch WinZip in the usual way, and WinZip will silently translate your Win-Zip commands into PKZip commands; PKZip will actually do the work for you.

## For More Information

The PKZip archive available on the Net includes several files containing documentation on PKZip and the four other programs that come with it. Each of these files has an extension of *.doc*, but don't be fooled into thinking they were prepared by a word processing program like Microsoft Word for Windows; they contain only text. As a result, you may find it convenient to rename PKZip's documentation files so they all have a *.txt* extension. That way, you can quickly and easily look at them using Notepad.

If, after installing PKZIP, you type the name of any of the five PKZip-related programs to a DOS prompt, you'll receive help on how to use that program. For example, if you just type

```
pkzip
```

to a DOS prompt, you'll receive a summary of how to run PKZip, and you'll be given the opportunity to see more detailed help on how to use the program.

## Registering PKZip

PKZip is a shareware program with a $47 registration fee for individual use. The length of the shareware trial period is unstated in the documentation, but PKWARE suggests you decide whether you want to keep PKZip within 30 days after installing it.

If you register PKZip, you receive a disk containing the latest version of the software, a professionally printed manual, one free software upgrade, premium access to a BBS for technical support, and, if you wish, support for special ZIP archive security features.

## LZH Files

File archives in the LZH format are produced by a freeware program called LHA. LHA was developed by Haruyasu Yoshizaki, and until relatively recently, the program was called LH. When MS-DOS 5.0 came out, however, it contained a command of its own called LH, so Yoshizaki renamed the program LHA to eliminate the conflict.

In view of the fact that LHA's author is Japanese, it is not surprising that LZH files are more common in Japan than they are elsewhere. However, the Net is global, so you may find yourself downloading files from Japan more frequently than you expect. If so, you'll be glad you have LHA and that WinZip knows how to use it.

LHA is distributed as a self-extracting archive, and you'll find a copy of the LHA SEA on the diskette that accompanies this book. Installation is simple:

1. **Create a directory and copy LHA from the diskette**: Create a new directory on your hard drive for LHA. We recommend you use *c:\lha*, and in the instructions that follow, we assume that's the directory you'll use. Copy the self-extracting archive *lha213.exe* from the *programs* directory of this book's diskette into *c:\lha*.

2. **Extract files**: In the File Manager, double-click on *c:\lha\lha213.exe*. The files contained inside the archive will be extracted onto your hard disk. Press F5 to make the File Manager update itself and show you these new files.

3. **Tell WinZip about LHA**: Start WinZip by double-clicking on its icon in the Program Manager
or by double-clicking on *c:\winzip\winzip.exe* in
the File Manager. After you acknowledge Win-
Zip's licensing agreement, you'll see WinZip's
main window.

Click on WinZip's **Options** menu, then select
**Program Locations...**, and you'll be presented
with WinZip's Program Locations dialog box. In
the *LHA* box, enter the location of the LHA program: *c:\lha\lha.exe*. Assuming you have *not*
installed PKZip, the middle part of the dialog box
will then look like this:

| | |
|---|---|
| PK**Z**IP: | |
| PK**U**NZIP: | |
| ZIP**2**EXE: | |
| **A**RJ | |
| **L**HA: | C:\LHA\LHA.EXE |
| AR**C** Extraction: | |
| **D**efault Association: | C:\WINDOWS\NOTEPAD.EXE |

Click on **OK** to close the dialog box, then exit
WinZip.

4. **Delete the unnecessary file**: You no longer
need the file *lha213.exe* that's in your *c:\lha*
directory; it's just a copy of the same file that's in
the *programs* directory of this book's diskette.
We recommend you conserve space on your hard
disk by deleting *c:\lha\lha213.exe*.

That's all you have to do to install LHA and to tell Win-
Zip about it. In the future, whenever you need to work
with LHA files, you can just launch WinZip in the usual
way, and WinZip will silently translate your WinZip commands into LHA commands; LHA will actually do the
work for you.

## For More Information

 LHA comes with three text files containing documentation. Unfortunately, none of them have the standard *.txt* file extension, and two of them have extensions that can be misleading to Windows users: *lha.hlp* is *not* a Windows help file, and *lha213.doc* is not a word-processing document. To be fair, LHA is designed for DOS, not Windows, and these file names make sense to DOS users. At any rate, we recommend you rename *lha.hlp*, *lha213.doc* and *history.eng* to have *.txt* extensions so you can easily view them with Notepad.

The files in which you are most likely to be interested are *lha.hlp* and *lha213.doc*. The former is a shorter "Help Guide," while the latter is a more complete manual. The file *history.eng* contains a history of changes to the program, and unless you really need to know about the problems that have been discovered and fixed since the program was first created, you are unlikely to be interested in this file.

If you give the simple command

```
lha
```

to a DOS prompt, you'll be presented with a summary of the program's options.

## Registering LHA

It's wonderful and it's true: LHA is freeware, so there is no need to register and no need to pay.

## ARJ Files

ARJ stands for "Archiver by Robert Jung," and the program you need to work with ARJ files is a shareware program called, appropriately enough, ARJ.

The archive containing ARJ comes with more than just the program WinZip uses. It also contains a whole host of DOS programs that collectively perform more archive-related tasks than you can shake a mouse at. As an added bonus, it comes with a jewel of a program called REARJ, which converts archive files in more than a half-dozen other formats into ARJ files. Such a capability can be a lifesaver if you come across an archive containing files you want, but you don't have a program that understands the archive's format.

ARJ is distributed as a self-extracting archive, and you'll find a copy of the ARJ SEA on the diskette that accompanies this book. Installation is easy:

1. **Create a directory and copy ARJ from the diskette**: Create a new directory on your hard drive for ARJ. We recommend you use *c:\arj*, and in the instructions that follow, we assume that's the directory you'll use. Copy the self-extracting archive *arj241a.exe* from the *programs* directory of this book's diskette into *c:\arj*.

2. **Extract files**: In the File Manager, double-click on *c:\arj\arj241a.exe*. The files contained inside the archive will be extracted onto your hard disk. Press F5 to make the File Manager update itself and show you these new files.

3. **Tell WinZip about ARJ**: Start WinZip by double-clicking on its icon in the Program Manager or by double-clicking on *c:\winzip\winzip.exe* in the File Manager. After you acknowledge WinZip's licensing agreement, you'll see WinZip's main window.

   Click on WinZip's **Options** menu, then select **Program Locations...**, and you'll be presented with WinZip's Program Locations dialog box. In the *ARJ* box, enter the location of the ARJ program:

*c:\arj\arj.exe*. Assuming you have already installed LHA but have *not* installed PKZip, the middle part of the dialog box will then look like this:

| | |
|---|---|
| PKZIP: | |
| PKUNZIP: | |
| ZIP2EXE: | |
| ARJ: | C:\ARJ\ARJ.EXE |
| LHA: | C:\LHA\LHA.EXE |
| ARC Extraction: | ⬦ |
| Default Association: | C:\WINDOWS\NOTEPAD.EXE |

Click on **OK** to close the dialog box, then exit WinZip.

4. **Delete the unnecessary file**: You no longer need the file *arj241a.exe* that's in your *c:\arj* directory; it's just a copy of the same file that's in the *programs* directory of this book's diskette. We recommend you conserve space on your hard disk by deleting *c:\arj\arj241a.exe*.

That's all you have to do to install ARJ and to tell Win-Zip about it. In the future, whenever you need to work with ARJ files, you can just fire up WinZip in the usual manner, and WinZip will silently translate your WinZip commands into ARJ commands; ARJ will actually do the work for you.

## *For More Information*

The ARJ archive contains over two dozen files, and more than half of them contain documentation. Such files end in *.doc*, but beware: they are best viewed with a program like Notepad, not with a high-powered word-processing program like Microsoft Word for Windows (whose files also typically end with *.doc*). As a result, you may find it convenient to rename ARJ's documentation files so they have a *.txt* extension.

The best place to start reading about ARJ are the files *readme.doc*, which summarizes the contents of the files in the archive, and *intro.doc*, which provides an overview of ARJ's basic capabilities. For detailed information, consult *arj.doc*, which is the complete User's Manual for the programs in the ARJ archive.

If you simply type

```
arj
```

to a DOS prompt, you'll receive a summary of how to run the program.

## Registering ARJ

The rules regarding registration of ARJ are best summarized in the file *license.doc*, which is part of the ARJ archive. In brief, registration is optional if your use of ARJ is strictly "non-commercial, non-business, non-institutional, non-government [and] personal."

Nonetheless, you are encouraged to pay the registration fee, which is $40 for individuals. Registration entitles you to free technical support, the ability to order ARJ upgrades directly from the author, and the opportunity to order source code (in the C programming language) for many of the programs distributed with ARJ (though not for ARJ itself). You also garner the satisfaction of supporting the shareware industry.

If you want to use ARJ to support any kind of commercial activity, ARJ is strictly shareware, and the trial period is 30 days. For details, read *license.doc*.

## ARC Files

The ARC archive format is an old-timer in the PC world, but it's no longer widely used. In fact, it's rare to find a new ARC file on the Net, because almost all archives these days are built in one of the newer formats, such as ZIP, LZH, and ARJ.

Still, ARC files used to be quite common, so you may run into one from time to time as you explore the Net. If you do, you'll want WinZip to be able to extract and uncompress the archive's contents, and for that you'll need a program that understands ARC files.

Unfortunately, there is no "standard" program on the Net for dealing with ARC files as there are for ZIP, LZH, and ARJ files. Instead, there are several programs that work with ARC files. (Most of the programs are rather old, much like ARC files themselves.) WinZip will let you use any of the following four:

- **ARC**: The original shareware program for creating and manipulating ARC archives, ARC is distributed by System Enhancement Associates, Inc. ARC can create new ARC archives as well as extract files from existing archives.

- **ARCE**: A freeware program that can only extract files from ARC archives; it can't create new archives. Written by Vernon Buerg, this program is fast, small, and free, and it's our recommendation for use with WinZip. If we'd been able to include it on the diskette that comes with this book, we'd have done so. Sometimes ARCE is known as **ARC-E**.

- **PKXARC**: Like ARCE, this is an extraction-only program. It was produced by the folks at PKWARE, Inc., until they abandoned the ARC format in favor of their own wildly successful ZIP format. PKXARC is shareware.

- **PKUNPAK**: Another extraction-only shareware program. It's also from PKWARE, Inc., but PKUN-PAK appears to be a bit more recent than PKX-ARC.

 It is difficult to describe exactly how to install these different programs, because one is distributed as an SEA, one as a ZIP file, and two are distributed as simple executable programs. However, the way to tell WinZip about the program you've got is the same in all four cases, and it involves but a single step.

For example, let's assume you've installed the ARCE program, and you've made sure it's on your DOS path. (If you don't know what your DOS path is, or if you're not sure how to add a program like ARCE to your path, consult your DOS documentation or give the command

```
help path
```

to access DOS's online documentation.) To tell WinZip to use ARCE for ARC files, you simply do this:

1. **Tell WinZip about ARCE**: Start WinZip by double-clicking on its icon in the Program Manager or by double-clicking on *c:\winzip\winzip.exe* in the File Manager. After you acknowledge WinZip's licensing agreement, you'll see WinZip's main window.

   Click on WinZip's **Options** menu, then select **Program Locations...**, and you'll be presented with WinZip's Program Locations dialog box. Click on the down-pointing arrow opposite the *ARC Extraction* box, and select **ARCE.COM** from the list. WinZip will automatically fill in the *ARC Extraction* field, and, assuming you have already installed LHA and ARJ but have not installed PKZip, the middle part of the dialog box will look like this:

| | |
|---|---|
| PK**Z**IP: | |
| PK**U**NZIP: | |
| ZIP**2**EXE: | |
| **A**RJ | C:\ARJ\ARJ.EXE |
| **L**HA: | C:\LHA\LHA.EXE |
| AR**C** Extraction: | ARCE.COM |
| **D**efault Association: | C:\WINDOWS\NOTEPAD.EXE |

Click on **OK** to close the dialog box, then exit WinZip.

For details on ARC, ARCE, PKXARC, and PKUNPAK, consult the documentation files that accompany those programs. For more information about using these programs with WinZip, read the "System Requirements" topic of WinZip's online documentation.

# Encoding and Decoding Files

In this chapter, we describe why it can be difficult to send many types of files through electronic mail or to post them to electronic bulletin boards, and we explain how *encoding* can be used to overcome the difficulty. We go on to introduce XferPro, a program we've included with this book so you can easily work with encoded files. We conclude this chapter with an explanation of how you can use XferPro to decode files with the mere double-click of a mouse button.

## Unprintable Characters and Electronic Mail

Electronic mail is often the most convenient way to move information between computers. If you want to send a file to someone over a network like the Internet, for example, electronic mail is often the easiest way to do it.

Unfortunately, most electronic mail systems are limited in the kinds of information they can carry. In particular, many electronic mail systems fail to behave properly unless you restrict yourself to only about half the characters that are available on your computer. The characters you are allowed to use happen to be those that you, as a human being, are likely to need, because they include all the letters, numbers, and punctuation marks on your keyboard. These are often called the *printable* characters. For sending messages in English (and many other natural languages), the restrictions on electronic mail are not likely to be noticeable.

Computers, however, are not human, and they make extensive use of the characters that electronic mail systems often prohibit. Such characters are commonly referred to as *unprintable* characters. Computer programs, for example, are filled with unprintable characters, as are file archives, formatted documents (such as those used by word processors like WordPerfect), and most files that contain sounds, images, and movies. In fact, *most* of the files on your computer probably contain characters that would make them unacceptable to many electronic mail programs.

What do you do, then, if you'd like to electronically mail a file containing unprintable characters to another person? For example, suppose you discover a file archive containing a nice shareware program, and you want to send a copy of the archive to a friend or colleague. What you'd like to do is just send an electronic mail message containing the archive, but such a message, chock full of unprintable characters as it would be, would almost certainly give your mail program the computer equivalent of indigestion — or worse. What you'd need would be a way to transform the archive into something you could mail, but that the recipient of your message could transform back into the original archive. That is, you'd need a way to translate a file containing unprintable characters (a *binary file*) into a file containing only printable characters (a *text file*), but you'd need to make sure the text file could be translated back into the original binary file.

The need to translate binary files into text files arises in more situations than you might imagine, because electronic mail systems are used to do more than just send messages back and forth between people. For example, one of the most attractive features of the Internet is its thousands of *newsgroups*. Each newsgroup is a separate electronic bulletin board devoted to a different topic, and each message that appears on a newsgroup is called a *posting*. Every day there are tens of thousands — possibly hundreds of thousands — of postings sent to Internet newsgroups, and each posting is treated like a piece of electronic mail. As such, postings must contain only printable characters, but the people making the postings are unwilling to be so constrained. They want to post programs, pictures, sounds, file archives, and other binary files, so they, too, require a way to translate files containing unprintable characters into text files that the Internet newsgroups are willing to accept.

## Encoding Binary Files

The solution to this problem is called *encoding*. You can encode a binary file, and the result will be a block of printable text. As you'll soon see, the resulting text won't make much sense to you, but you can safely send it via electronic mail or post it to a newsgroup, and once the encoded information has reached its destination, the receiver can *decode* it to convert it back to its original binary form.

There are several encoding techniques for binary files. The most common is called *uuencoding*, which stands for Unix-to-Unix encoding. This technique allows you to send data between computers that use the ASCII character set, and that's almost all the computers you're likely to run into these days. All PCs and all Macintoshes, for example, use ASCII.

Another technique, called *xxencoding*, allows you to send data between computers, even if one or both of the computers isn't using the ASCII character set. The most common alternative character set is EBCDIC, which is used by IBM mainframe computers.

If you can't tell your ASCIIs from your EBCDICs (and who can?), don't worry. Uuencoding works most of the time, and when it doesn't, xxencoding will work. At any rate, as a downloader, you don't need to concern yourself with learning how to determine what kind of encoding to use, because you'll be downloading files that have already been encoded. Your only interest will be in decoding the files, regardless of whether they are uuencoded or xxencoded or have been encoded in some other way.

## Recognizing a Uuencoded File

Uuencoding is far and away the most common encoding technique, so it's worth your while to learn how to recognize a file that's been uuencoded. For example, an electronic mail message containing a uuencoded file looks like that shown in Figure 8; an Internet newsgroup posting looks quite similar.

Such a message is strikingly recognizable. The bulk of the message is a large block of text consisting of uppercase letters, spaces, and punctuation marks only, and all the lines in the block of text are the same length. Above the block is a line like this,

```
begin 644 BANNER21.ZIP
```

which tells the decoding program that a block of encoded text is about to begin and suggests that the decoded information be placed in a file called *BANNER21.ZIP*. Because you are now familiar with how a program's version number is often made part of the name of the archive containing that program (see the explanation beginning on page 40 if you don't recall how this is done), you recognize that the electronic mail message above contains a uuencoded ZIP archive containing version 2.1 of a program called BANNER. Such a program might be designed to generate banners for printing on fan-fold paper.

(In the above message, the number 644 between the "begin" and the name of the encoded file tells Unix com-

```
From: programs@programs-are-us.com
To: downloader-pro
Date: Mon, 11 Jul 94 23:50:25 EDT
Subject: New UUEncoded Program

Here's the new uuencoded program we were talking about. We hope you
like it.

Alexander

begin 644 BANNER21.ZIP
MO?1)T/X7B@QY3'CPYCK?B3N'P6C2^3D'7?-]J-T:U:.*35OO0-('4A>:98X8
MV>5FX0'DG[#F^-78O0AOJTTK*>EY"<<-(GAKV]"U#7J\3=-PE4XG29H9H9=OYZ!
M?'`61N+-!=11HW5UZ]]11UIG4\UE\++`Z8L'8G6:3ADZ''M7[_'-G16.'MMA:;E^'G,7
MPIU5U5N5&&/P'`P-D+`0&3N](%2Z-W.>|-T-,<6&%E<Y#-F-YA&<#16U!@;E@N&#
MV>?U$'(O'0I>=Jw18qJ_
```

```
M#7(JZ^QOB^.+RC>S?PQ'b....~L?DA0[6GH':=I8+M8\WONNnP()UZ+T7X,
MQ<9@S/#**XKQ99(@WAFU((['<BQ0)%]_75Z(10JR01(JT'&V7O%4*'[4.'!!{[?
...
end
```

Figure 8

puters what kind of protection the decoded file should have. The number is not particularly meaningful for Windows users, and most decoding programs for Windows ignore it.)

At the end of the encoded information is the single line

```
end
```

which, naturally enough, tells the decoding program that it has reached the end of the encoded information.

If you edit a file containing uuencoded data (which we do *not* recommend), don't remove the lines containing the "begin" and the "end". If you do, the decoding program will be unable to make sense of the file you ask it to decode, and you will be unable to recover the original binary file that's encoded in the text. Similarly, be sure to avoid modifying the uuencoded text itself. If you change it *in any way*, the decoding program will almost certainly give up in despair when it tries to recreate the binary file represented by that text.

## Using XferPro to Work with Encoded Files

Encoding and decoding files is easy, if you've got the right program to do the job, and we've included the right program with this book. It's a shareware program called XferPro, and it was developed by Bruce Sabalas-key. Though the documentation that comes with the program is somewhat terse, the program itself is a life-saver. It's flexible, it's powerful, and you don't have to be a genius to learn how to use it. With XferPro, you decode files by just double-clicking on them in the File Manager.

### Installing XferPro

Installing programs that are distributed in the form of ZIP files is a simple process, now that you know how to run WinZip, and XferPro is such a program. XferPro complicates matters slightly by coming with its own Setup program that you need to run after extracting XferPro from the ZIP file, but installation of XferPro is still easy.

1. **Create directories**: Create a new directory, *c:\xferpro,* on your hard disk. This is where you'll install XferPro. You may use a different directory for the installation if you like, but in the instructions that follow, we assume you're going to install in *c:\xferpro.* You'll also need a directory on your hard disk where you can store temporary files. We assume you'll use *c:\temp,* and you should create this directory if it does not already exist. Of course, you are free to use any directory you like for temporary files, but in the instructions that follow, we assume you'll use *c:\temp.*

2. **Extract files**: From the *programs* directory of this book's diskette, copy *xferp100.zip* into the *c:\temp* directory you created. In the File Manager, double-click on *c:\temp\xferp100.zip* to run WinZip on it. In WinZip, click on **Extract** to bring up the File Extraction dialog box. (Be sure to use the **Extract** button instead of the **Check-Out** button. In this case, you don't want WinZip to create a Program Manager group for the files being extracted. XferPro comes with its own Setup program, and that program will add Xfer-Pro to the Program Manager for you.)

   If it's not there already, enter *c:\temp* in the *Extract To* box. The dialog box will look like this:

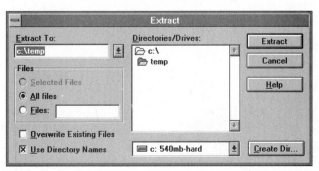

   Click on **Extract** to extract all the files. Exit Win-Zip.

3. **Run Setup**: Use the File Manager to double-click on *setup.exe* in *c:\temp*; this will run Xfer-Pro's Setup program. When Setup asks you to specify the drive and directory for the installation, enter *c:\xferpro*, then click on **Install**. When Setup asks you for the name of the Program Manager group where it should add XferPro's icons, specify the group you prefer or let Setup use the default group of *Utilities*. If you don't already have this group and you let Setup create it, you'll find a new Program Manager group that looks like this when Setup is done:

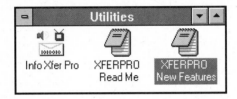

4. **Set up File Manager associations**: Set up File Manager associations so that the following extensions are associated with *c:\xferpro\xfer-pro.exe*: *.uu*, *.uue*, *.xx*, *.xxe*, and *.mme*. If you've forgotten how to set up File Manager associations, you can refresh your memory with the discussion that begins on page 43.

5. **Delete unnecessary files**: You no longer need the XferPro-related files that are located in *c:\temp*, so we recommend you conserve disk space by deleting them.

That's it. XferPro is now installed.

## Decoding Files

You'll most frequently wish to use XferPro after you download a uuencoded file. Such a file might be an electronic mail message you receive that contains a uuencoded file (see page 85), or it might be a file you find on a bulletin board or in a newsgroup posting that contains uuencoded information.

Decoding such a file is simplicity itself. Provided you've given the file a name that ends with *.uue* or *.uu*, all you need to do is double-click on the file in the File Manager, and XferPro will automatically be launched to decode the file. For example, if you double-click on the file *earth.uue* you'll find in the *samples* directory of this book's diskette (this file contains a uuencoded image of the planet Earth), XferPro will present you with the following dialog box, which you can use to specify the name of the file where you'd like the decoded output to be stored:

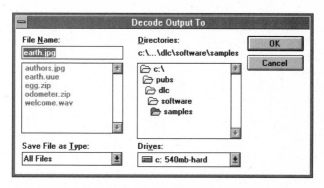

The file name that XferPro puts in the *File Name* box is the suggested name found inside the uuencoded file itself, but you can change the name of the output file if you wish.

After you've specified the output file and clicked on **OK**, XferPro begins the process of decoding the file, and it shows you its progress through a bar graph that looks like this:

When the decoding is done, the XferPro window simply goes away, and you can then use the File Manager to verify that the decoded file is present on your disk in the location you specified. In this case, you'll end up with a file called *earth.jpg*. You'll learn how to view the picture in that file in Chapter 6.

## Decoding Multi-Part Files

Sometimes an encoded file will be broken into two or more pieces, and the pieces will be stored in separate files. The most common reason for doing this is to satisfy size restrictions on electronic mail messages or on newsgroup or bulletin board postings. Many electronic mail and bulletin board systems put an upper limit on the size of the messages or postings they'll allow, and often these limits are too small to accommodate files that have been encoded. The easiest way to get around such limits is to break an encoded file into pieces, mail or post each piece separately, and then have the person receiving the pieces or downloading the postings reassemble the pieces after the fact. It is not uncommon to find files in Internet newsgroups that have been broken up into a half-dozen or more separate encoded files in this way.

Unfortunately, if you are the person who wants to reconstruct the original encoded file so you can decode it, the fact that you have to knit together lots of little encoded files complicates your life. You have to make sure you have all the pieces, you put the pieces back together in the right order, and you don't make any mistakes when you combine the pieces. Such work is not only error-prone, it's just plain boring.

Fortunately, XferPro knows how to handle encoded files that have been broken into pieces, so all you have to do is tell XferPro the names of the files that contain the pieces, and it will automatically verify that all the pieces are present, will arrange them in the right order, and will merge them correctly. In short, XferPro can handle multi-part encoded files as easily as it handles single-part encoded files.

As an example, let's suppose a friend of yours, while exploring the Net, found the Odometer program we discussed earlier, and she wanted you to try it out. Let's further suppose the two of you live on different continents, so the easiest (and fastest) way for her to send the program to you would be by electronic mail. To do that, she'd uuencode *odometer.zip*, and she'd send the resulting file to you.

However, let's also suppose her mail program balked at large messages, so your friend was forced to break the uuencoded ZIP file into three pieces and send each piece to you in a separate message. Your job would then be to reconstitute the original ZIP file from the three email messages you received.

To do so, you would follow these steps:

1. **Place the encoded files in a directory for temporary files**: If you didn't already have a directory you use for temporary files, you'd create *c:\temp* for that purpose. You'd then download the three email messages your friend sent you, and you'd store them in *c:\temp* as *odomail1.uue*, *odomail2.uue*, and *odomail3.uue*.

2. **Launch XferPro**: You'd launch XferPro by double-clicking on its icon in the Program Manager or by double-clicking on *xferpro.exe* in the File Manager. You would *not* double-click on one of the *.uue* files you just placed in *c:\temp*, because that would decode only that single file, and you'd want to decode all three files together. After all, XferPro can't regenerate *odometer.zip* from the three electronic mail messages unless it knows about all three messages.

3. **Confirm correct decoding configuration**: You'd select **Decode...** from the **Configure** menu to bring up the Decode Configure dialog box. You'd make sure that *Automatic Detection of Decode File Format* and *Decode Multiple Input Files as 1 File* were both checked. If they weren't, you'd click on them both:

```
┌─────────────────────────────────────────────────────────────┐
│                    Decode Configuration                       │
├─────────────────────────────────────────────────────────────┤
│  ☒ Automatic Detection of Decode File Format                  │
│  ┌─Decode File Format────────────────────────┐               │
│  │  ● Single File          ○ X-File-Name Format│  ┌──────────┐│
│  │  ○ SIMTEL Format        ○ UUXFER Format     │  │ Configure ││
│  │  ○ Comp.binaries Format ○ Wincode Format    │  └──────────┘│
│  │  ○ Alt.binaries Format 1 ○ POST             │  ┌──────────┐│
│  │  ○ Alt.binaries Format 2 ○ xmitBin          │  │  Save     ││
│  │  ○ Alt.binaries Format 3 ○ bitftp           │  └──────────┘│
│  │  ○ Alt.binaries Format 4 ○ MIME             │  ┌──────────┐│
│  │  ○ UNIX shell archive    ○ R.E.M. Format    │  │  Cancel   ││
│  └─────────────────────────────────────────────┘  └──────────┘│
│  ┌─Decode Method──────────┐                       ┌──────────┐│
│  │  ● Based on File Name   │                       │   Help    ││
│  │  ○ UU                   │                       └──────────┘│
│  │  ○ XX                   │  ☒ Decode Multiple Input Files as 1 File
│  │  ○ MIME                 │  ☒ Test Checksum Data if Present
│  └────────────────────────┘                                   │
└─────────────────────────────────────────────────────────────┘
```

Then you'd click on **Configure** to close the dialog box.

4. **Specify files to be decoded**: You'd select **Decode...** from XferPro's **File** menu to bring up the Decode dialog box. You'd select *c:\temp* for the value of the *Directories* box, and then you'd select *all three* odometer *.uue* files listed in the *File Name* listing. One way to do this would be to click once on each *.uue* file while holding down the Ctrl key. All three files would then be highlighted, and all three would be present in the *File Name* box. The dialog box would look like this:

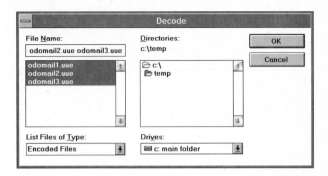

You'd click on **OK**.

5.  **Specify a file name for the decoded infor-
    mation**: XferPro would start merging the individ-
    ual *.uue* files and decoding the original binary file.
    Soon it would find the suggested file name for the
    decoded data (recall from page 84) that this file
    name is present in all uuencoded files), and you'd
    see the dialog box for specifying the output file
    name:

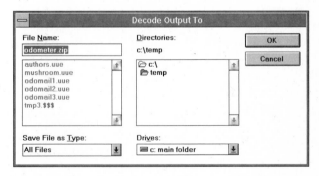

You'd probably click on **OK** to accept the default
name of *odometer.zip*, but you could, of course,
specify a different name if you wanted to.

XferPro would then complete its decoding of
*odometer.zip*, and when it was done, XferPro
would disappear. You would then be free to dou-

ble-click on *odometer.zip* so you could extract the files within it using WinZip.

## Configuring XferPro

XferPro allows you to configure its decoding behavior, its encoding behavior, and certain aspects of its general behavior. You don't have to configure XferPro, of course. If you like, you can rely on the program's default behavior, and that will do what you want in most situations. (That's why it's the default behavior.)

Nevertheless, we've found it useful to configure XferPro's decoding and encoding behavior, and we suggest you configure XferPro this way, too, at least until you have a bit more experience with the program.

### *Configuring XferPro's Decoding Behavior*

When you select **Decode...** from the **Configure** menu, you are presented with this dialog box:

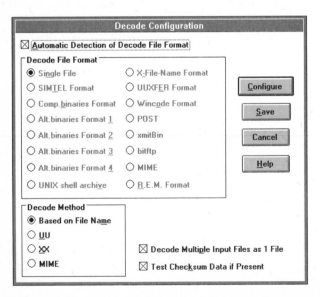

We recommend you fill it out as shown. These options tell XferPro the following:

- *Automatic Detection of Decode File Format* tells it to try to automatically figure out the format of an encoded file. XferPro understands 16 different formats, and it's a lot easier to let XferPro figure out the format of a file than it is to try to figure it out yourself.

- *Decode Method Based on File Name* tells it to look at a file's extension to determine which of XferPro's three primary decoding methods it should employ. The alternative is to always use a particular decoding method, and this is less flexible than choosing the method based on the file name.

- *Decode Multiple Input Files as 1 File* tells it to knit multi-part encoded files together into a single output file, if it can. You won't truly understand how useful this feature is until the first time you're presented with a uuencoded file that's been broken into seven or eight different pieces. *Then* you'll truly understand.

- *Test Checksum Data if Present* tells XferPro to check for errors in the encoded file, provided error-detection information is present.

For details on the options presented in this dialog box, click **Help** to access XferPro's online documentation.

## Configuring XferPro's Encoding Behavior

To configure the encoding process, select **Encode...** from the **Configure** menu. You will see this dialog box, which allows you to specify the details of how you'd like your files to be encoded:

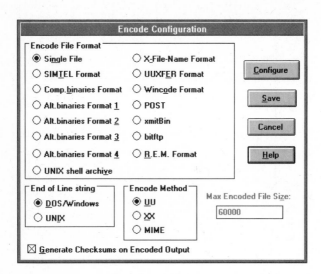

As a downloader, you won't need to worry about this box very much, because you'll be spending your time decoding files, not encoding them. If, however, you decide you'd like to give unto the Net as you have received, you'll need to know how to encode files for uploading, and we recommend you fill out the dialog box as shown above. It specifies the following:

- *Encode File Format: Single File* tells XferPro to generate a single encoded file, even if it's very large. XferPro can also generate multi-part files; consult the program's online help for an explanation of how to do this. (Don't worry, it's not hard.)

- *End of Line string: DOS/Windows* tells XferPro to prepare the encoding using DOS/Windows conventions. Since your machine is a PC running Windows, this option is natural.

- *Encode Method: UU* tells XferPro to employ uuencoding as the encoding method of choice. Uuencoding is the most common encoding format, the

one understood by the largest number of other programs, so you should use it whenever you can.

For further information on the options presented in this
dialog box, click on its **Help** button.

## For More Information

 The foregoing discussion of XferPro has
only scratched the surface of its capabilities, and we encourage you to familiar-
ize yourself with its many other features.
Like all good Windows programs, Xfer-
Pro has extensive online documentation
available through the **Help** item of its menu bar. You
can also peruse the online documentation directly by
double-clicking on the *xferpro.hlp* file in the File Manager; this eliminates the need to actually run XferPro
when all you want to do is read about it. You can also
order a printed copy of the XferPro online documentation when you send in your registration fee.

## Registering XferPro

XferPro offers an unusually generous 60-day trial
period, after which you are required to either register
your copy of the program or get rid of it. After using it
for two months, however, we're inclined to think you'll
have grown accustomed to its presence.

When you send in the utterly reasonable $10 registra-
tion fee, you'll receive a special password that permanently disables the nagware aspects of the program, and
for an additional $6, you'll also receive a printed manual
and a diskette containing the latest version of XferPro.
Registered users are also entitled to free technical support, including support via electronic mail. For all the
details, consult XferPro's online documentation.

# 6

# Images, Sounds, and Movies

You have probably heard of multimedia computing. That's where computers do more than just put windows on the screen; they also display pictures, play music, even show movies. If you're connected to the Net, and especially if your PC has a sound card, multimedia computing is here now, and you can be a part of it — *if* you know how to work with the pictures, sounds, and movies you can download. This chapter will tell you *everything* you need to know.

## Images and Your PC

When a picture shows up on a computer screen, it's usually referred to as an *image*. Most images get into a computer by having someone take a photograph, drawing, or some other kind of picture and *scan* it using a *scanner*, which is a device that is similar to a copy machine. Instead of producing a copy, however, a scanner produces a file containing an image of the picture that was scanned (see Figure 9).

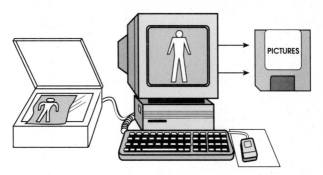

Figure 9

When a picture is scanned, the scanner divides it up into a very fine grid of squares, and the color of each square — each *pixel (picture element)* — is recorded. If there is more than one color in a pixel, the scanner chooses one and records that color for the entire pixel:

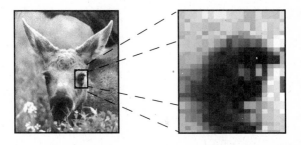

When scanning a picture, the finer the grid, the better the resulting image. Of course, the finer the grid, the more pixels there are in an image, hence the larger the computer file needed to store the image.

When an image is displayed on your computer monitor, each pixel in the image is displayed as a point on your screen. As a rule, the more colors your monitor can display at a time, the better the images will look. A reasonable color monitor can display at least 256 colors at a time. Fancier monitors can display about 16 million colors at a time; such monitors can display images with almost photographic quality. A few monitors can show only 16 colors at a time. If you're unfortunate enough to have such a monitor, you are likely to be disappointed in the quality of the images (and movies) you display, because the world has a lot more than 16 colors in it! On the other hand, don't worry if your monitor can show only 256 colors, because such a monitor will display images perfectly adequately. Besides, as you will soon discover, most images on the Net use no more than 256 colors anyway.

 Many computer systems can be configured in different ways, with some configurations allowing more colors than others. If you have such a system, and if you are currently using a configuration that displays fewer than 256 colors, we recommend you consider reconfiguring your system to display more colors. Unfortunately, there is no standard way to do this, so you'll have to consult the documentation that came with your computer and monitor to determine whether you can reconfigure your system to display more colors, and, if so, exactly how you do it.

## Images on the Net

The Net is filled with downloadable images, and that's good. Unfortunately, the files containing those images are in literally dozens of formats (see Appendix B), and from a downloader's point of view, that's not so good. The problem is that you can't look at an image unless you have a program on your PC that understands the format in which that image is stored.

Fortunately, almost all the images on the Net are stored in one of two formats, either the GIF format or the JPEG format. The GIF (Graphics Interchange Format) format was developed by CompuServe, but it's now used just about everywhere. GIF files generally have the extension *.gif*. JPEG stands for the Joint Photographic Experts Group, and that's the group that originally developed the JPEG format. JPEG files usually have the file extension *.jpg*.

The most interesting difference between these two formats is the kind of information they store about an image. A GIF file stores a color for each pixel in the image. However, each GIF image is limited to a total of 256 different colors. A GIF representation of a picture, then, is really just an approximation of the picture, because the number of different colors in a picture is essentially unlimited, while the GIF representation must make do with only 256 colors. Nevertheless, GIF files yield images that, to the human eye, are close to the original, and GIF images displayed on a computer screen can look very nice indeed.

The JPEG approach is completely different. A JPEG file stores information about color *changes* in an image, not information about the colors themselves. A JPEG file doesn't store a color for every pixel in an image, and, as a result, the image generated from a JPEG file is not necessarily pixel-for-pixel identical with the original picture. JPEG is therefore considered to be a *lossy* representation for images, because it loses information about an image when it stores it in a file. A GIF representation, in contrast, is called *lossless*, because it stores information about every pixel in an image.

Interestingly, although the pixels in a JPEG image may not have precisely the same colors as those in the original picture, a JPEG image often *looks* better than an image generated from a lossless representation like GIF. There are two reasons for this. The first is that JPEG images are not limited to 256 colors — they can use as many colors as they like. The second has to do with the way our eyes work.

The human eye is an edge-seeking and change-seeking device. It perceives *changes* in color, in shape, and especially in brightness more easily than it perceives colors themselves. As long as a computer-generated image has variations in brightness that are similar to the original picture, the human eye will see the two as identical or as almost identical. In general, JPEG images do this better than GIF images.

The GIF and JPEG formats automatically compress the information they store about images, so it's not worth trying to compress them further. If you like, of course, you can use WinZip to turn them into ZIP files, but you'll find that the savings you get are minimal. JPEG files are usually compressed more tightly than GIF files. As a result, a JPEG file for an image tends to be only one-fourth to one-third the size of a GIF file for the same image. On the Net, GIF and JPEG files are usually stored as individual *.gif* and *.jpg* files; only rarely are they found in archives.

Currently, GIF files are more common on the Net than JPEG files, but this is beginning to change. Because JPEG files tend to be smaller than GIF files and because JPEG images often look better than GIF images, there is a compelling case for using JPEG instead of GIF. In the long run, it's likely that JPEG will become the dominant image format on the Net.

## Using LView Pro to Work with Images

We have included with this book a very nice program for viewing and editing images. This program, LView Pro, can display images in four different formats, including those in the GIF and JPEG formats. LView Pro also gives you the ability to do neat tricks, such as resizing an image, reversing an image so it appears as a photographic negative, converting an image from one format to another, and adjusting an image's color tones, contrast and brightness.

LView Pro was written by Leonardo Haddad Loureiro and is freeware for personal, non-commercial use. We like the price, but we especially like the fact that it's a versatile and professional piece of software.

## Installing LView Pro

LView Pro is distributed as a ZIP file, so you can install LView Pro using WinZip. Just follow these steps:

1. **Create directories**: Create a new directory *c:\lviewpro* on your hard disk. This is where you'll install LView Pro. You may use a different directory for the installation, if you like, but in the instructions that follow, we assume you're going to install in *c:\lviewpro*. You'll also need a directory on your hard disk where you can store temporary files. We assume you'll use *c:\temp*, and you should create this directory if it does not already exist. Of course, you are free to use any directory you like for temporary files, but in the instructions that follow, we assume you'll use *c:\temp*.

2. **Extract files and create a Program Manager group**: From the *programs* directory of this book's diskette, copy *lviewp18.zip* into *c:\temp*. In the File Manager, double-click on *c:\temp-\lviewp18.zip* to run WinZip on it. In WinZip, click on **CheckOut** to bring up the CheckOut dialog box. Enter *c:\lviewpro* in the *Directory* box, and check the two boxes at the bottom of the window. When you're done, the dialog box should look like this:

---

| CheckOut | |
|---|---|
| All files will be extracted to the specified directory, and a program group will be built. | **OK** |
| Directory: `c:\lviewpro` | **Cancel** |
| Group Name: `LVIEWP18` | **Help** |
| Maximum Icons: `20` | |
| ☒ Create Icons For Programs And Documents Only | |
| ☒ Run Virus Scanner | |
| Caution: any files in the specified directory and icons in the specified program group will be replaced. | |

As shown, the dialog box tells WinZip to scan the files in the LView Pro archive for viruses. In this case, it's not really necessary, because the files on this book's diskette were checked for viruses before they were approved for distribution. Still, it's a good idea to get into the habit of scanning all new programs for viruses during installation, so you might want to take this opportunity to get some practice. If not, just uncheck the *Run Virus Scanner* box. Of course, you can only scan for viruses if you've got a virus-scanning program installed on your computer.

Click on **OK** to have WinZip extract the files from the archive and to create a new Program Manager group containing icons for LView Pro and its documentation. The new group will look like this:

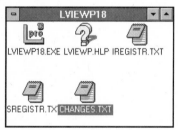

In the WinZip window, select **Close Archive** from the **File** menu, then click on **No** when you are prompted with this:

Exit WinZip.

3. **Set up File Manager associations**: Associate the following file extensions with *c:\lview-pro\lviewp18.exe*: *.jpg*, *.gif*, *.bmp*, and *.tga*. For instructions on setting up File Manager associations, see page 43.

4. **Delete unnecessary file**: You no longer need the file *c:\temp\lviewp18.zip*, because it's just a copy of a file that's in the *programs* directory of this book's diskette. We recommend you delete *c:\temp\lviewp18.zip* to save disk space.

Now give yourself a pat on the back — you've just installed LView Pro.

## Viewing Images with LView Pro

The most common way to run LView Pro is to simply double-click on a file in the File Manager that has one of the extensions you've associated with LView Pro. When you do, LView Pro will display the image contained in the file. This makes it easy to take a look at pictures you download.

However, producing a picture on your screen from the information in a file requires a fair amount of work on the part of your computer, so don't be surprised if some time — perhaps 30 seconds or more — elapses between the time you double-click on an image file and the time LView Pro puts the image in that file on your screen. Such a delay is normal. In general, the larger the image, the longer the delay. JPEG files, because of their high compression, tend to take longer to display than images stored in less compressed formats, such as GIF.

For example, if you double-click on *authors.jpg* in the *samples* directory of this book's diskette, you'll have to wait a bit before being presented with this image of *The Downloader's Companion*'s authors:

The two columns of buttons running along the right-hand side of the image make up the LView Pro *toolbar*, and we'll have much more to say about it shortly.

If you double-click on a file containing a relatively small image, LView Pro may take on a slightly different appearance, one where it abbreviates each of its menu bar entries. For instance, if you double-click on the file *leaves.bmp* in your Windows directory (which is usually *c:\windows*), LView Pro may come up like this, with its menu bar entries abbreviated to their first letters (**F** for **File**, **E** for **Edit**, etc.):

In this picture, we've omitted LView Pro's toolbar, but if you try this example on your computer (which we encourage you to do), you'll find that the toolbar is still present.

You don't have to have a file containing an image to run LView Pro. You can also double-click on its Program Manager icon or on its name in the File Manager, in which case you'll be presented with the LView Pro window and toolbar, but no image. Instead, you'll see a gray rectangle where an image would normally be displayed, and you'll get a toolbar that looks a bit different from the one you see when you display an image; we'll have more to say about this modified toolbar in a moment:

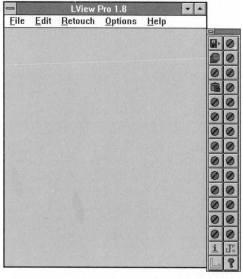

If LView Pro is running, and you'd like to have it display a different image from the one it's currently showing (if, in fact, it's showing an image at all), you can do that by simply opening a file containing the image you want to see. To open such a file, just do what you usually do in Windows applications to open a file: click on the **File** menu, then select **Open...** and use the resulting dialog box to specify the directory and name of the file you'd like to open. LView Pro will then display the image stored in that file.

# The LView Pro Toolbar

LView Pro can do much more than just show pretty pictures. It can also let you edit such pictures. The **Retouch** menu, in particular, is filled with commands for modifying the appearance of an image. If you're serious about editing images, however, constantly having to return to the menu bar can be annoying and can decrease your productivity.

This is where the toolbar comes in. Each button in the toolbar is a shortcut for a particular LView Pro command. Lest you wonder what the different buttons mean, we have prepared the following summary:

| | |
|---:|:---|
| Open File | Save File |
| Multiple Open | Undo |
| Cut | Copy |
| Paste | Crop |
| Resize | Add Text |
| Flip Horizontal | Flip Vertical |
| Rotate Left | Rotate Right |
| Gamma Correction | Color Balance |
| Contrast Enhance | HSV Adjust |
| YCbCr Adjust | Interactive RGB |
| Exp Enhance | Log Enhance |
| SineH Enhance | Grayscale |
| Negative | Image Filters |
| Palette Entry | Full Screen |
| Interface Options | JPEG I/O Options |
| About LView Pro | Help |

Sometimes only some of these commands make sense for the current image. For example, the **Undo** command makes sense only if you have issued a command that can be undone. Buttons which correspond to commands that don't make sense for the current image are depicted like this:

You should think of such buttons as meaning the same thing as a menu command that's grayed out. The command is still there, but you can't use it in the current context.

If you look again at the toolbar on page 107, you'll see that most of the toolbar buttons are disabled. This is because most toolbar commands affect the image being displayed, so they make sense only when LView Pro is displaying an image. On page 107, no image is being displayed.

## Customizing LView Pro for Your Monitor

LView Pro provides a great number of commands that let you adjust the color of an image, as well as its brightness, its contrast, and several other factors that affect its appearance. You need these capabilities, because PC monitors and video drivers vary widely in their characteristics. As a result, no picture can hope to look the same on all PCs unless the program displaying the image allows itself to be customized to take into account the individual characteristics of the computer system on which it is running. Without such customizations, an image may appear brighter on some monitors than on others. It may look washed out on one monitor, but clear and bright on another. It may have crisp, well-defined edges on some PCs, but look blurred on others.

The commands offered by LView Pro afford you the opportunity to discover which adjustments are appropriate for your particular computer system. By experimenting with the program's commands, you can identify the factors that are most important in producing well-balanced color images on your screen.

Of course, you don't have to fine-tune LView Pro if you don't want to. In most cases, you'll find that it displays images perfectly acceptably without your having to do a thing. That means you can spend more time trolling the Net for interesting images and less time worrying about things like what it means to adjust an image's YCbCr value.

## Converting Image Files to Other Formats

Sometimes you have an image in one format, but it would be more convenient to have it in a different format. For example, you might download a GIF file from the Net, but decide you'd like to store it as a JPEG file in order to save disk space. Or you might have a picture in JPEG format that you'd like to save as a *.bmp* file so you can tell Windows' Control Panel to use it to wallpaper your desktop.

Converting files from one format to another is easy. All you need to do is bring up the image in LView Pro, then save the image in a file with the extension associated with the desired format. For example, this is how you'd produce a GIF file containing the image stored in *authors.jpg* from this book's diskette:

1. **Launch LView Pro**: In the File Manager, double-click on *authors.jpg*. This will cause LView Pro to display the image in the file (as shown on page 106).

2. **Specify a new file name**: Select **Save as...** from the **File** menu, and use the resulting dialog box to specify a file name with a *.gif* extension. For example, to save the image as a GIF file in *c:\authors.gif*, you'd fill out the dialog box like this:

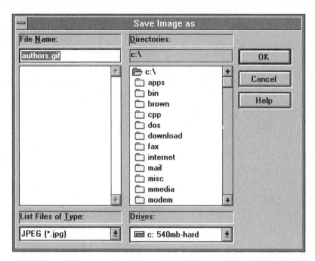

That's it. If you like, you can reassure yourself that the images in *authors.jpg* and *authors.gif* are the same by displaying each in LView Pro. You can see that they're in different formats by looking at their sizes: *authors.gif* will be about four times as big as *authors.jpg*.

## For More Information

The brief description of LView Pro presented in this chapter barely begins to describe its capabilities. You can't really appreciate all the things it can do until you've perused its online documentation.

To view that documentation, either double-click on *c:\lviewpro\lviewp.hlp* in the File Manager or select **Help** from LView Pro's menu bar. If you'd prefer a somewhat less intense introduction to its capabilities, start with the appropriately entitled *readme.1st*, which is located in *c:\lviewpro* (unless you installed LView Pro in a different directory).

## Registering LView Pro

Perhaps the best thing about LView Pro is that it's *free* for what the licensing agreement calls "leisure purposes." If all you plan to do is use LView Pro for your own personal enjoyment, you can sit back, relax, and never worry about having to shell out a dime for the program.

On the other hand, if you'd like to use LView Pro in any kind of commercial activity, you are obliged to register your copy of the program after the 20-day shareware trial period has expired. You may also wish to register your copy of the program if you're a power user and would like to get a copy of LView Pro that is optimized for higher performance under Windows NT or Win32s or on an Intel i486 or Pentium processor. (If that last sentence sounded like Greek to you, you're not a power user, and you don't need to worry about it.) The registration fee is $30.

For the full story on registration, consult the topic "Licensing, Registration and Distribution" in the LView Pro online documentation, and read the file *iregistr.txt* that's part of the LView Pro archive.

## Sounds and Your PC

Sounds, as they are heard in everyday life, are by nature an *analog* phenomenon. Most computers, on the other hand, are prepared to deal only with *digital* information.

For many years, this chasm between the analog nature of sounds and the digital nature of computers meant that sounds and computers were rarely found together. The success of the (digital) compact disk for recording music, however, led to a transformation of the audio industry. These days, sounds and computers are not just commonly found together, they are all but inseparable.

Still, most sounds originate in an analog form. For example, the sounds of voices and the sounds of musical

An ADC Converts Analog Sounds to Digital Sounds

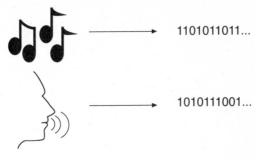

1101011011...

1010111001...

Figure 10

A DAC Converts Digital Sounds to Analog Sounds

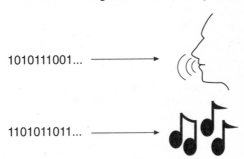

1010111001...

1101011011...

Figure 11

instruments are both analog sounds. To make such sounds acceptable to computers, they must be transformed into the digital form that computers require. This transformation is performed by a device called an analog-to-digital converter, or ADC.

An ADC takes an analog sound and converts it into a digital form, which is essentially a long series of ones and zeros. The ones and zeros shown in Figure 10 are what a computer actually manipulates. Ones and zeros are fine for machines, but if we are to hear sounds represented in that way, they must be converted back into their analog form, because that is the only form in which our ears can hear them. A digital-to-analog converter (DAC) performs this trick (see Figure 11).

This is where the sound card in your computer comes in. A PC sound card contains the ADC and DAC circuitry necessary to give your computer the abilities to record sounds and to replay them. Sound cards have many more capabilities, including the ability to play music and connect to devices like CD-ROM drives and synthesizer equipment. However, the only capability that concerns us here is their ability to play sounds you download from the Net, and all sound cards give you that.

## Sounds on the Net

Just as images on the Net come in different formats, so, too, may sounds be stored in different ways. Of the competing formats for sound files on PCs, two stand out as being particularly common. These are the VOC format and the WAV format.

The VOC format was designed by Creative Labs for its Sound Blaster audio card, and it soon became an unofficial standard for DOS programs. Compared to later formats, it is limited in both the duration and range of sounds it can represent. VOC files may be no more than 16 megabytes in size, and they represent sounds using only an eight-bit sample size. The technical details of this sample size are not particularly important, but it's worth knowing that this sample size prevents VOC files from representing sounds with the same fidelity as a compact disk. VOC files generally have the extension .*voc*.

VOC files are relatively plentiful on the Net, but they are outnumbered by WAV files. Such files, which have the extension .*wav*, contain sounds in the WAV format that was developed by Microsoft for use with Windows. This format supports sample sizes of both eight and 16 bits, and a 16-bit sample size is what is necessary to store sounds with the same fidelity as a compact disk. At their best, then, WAV files sound better than VOC files, sometimes much better.

There's no free lunch, however. The larger the sample size, the bigger the file, so a WAV representation of a sound using a 16-bit sample size is usually about twice as big as the corresponding VOC file. Furthermore, playing a WAV file may put more of a burden on your computer than playing a VOC file, because there's twice as much information to be processed.

Nevertheless, the WAV format has become *the* sound format of choice for Windows programmers. Virtually all Windows applications with multimedia capabilities support it, and there are a number of DOS applications that can play WAV files, too.

## Using WPLAny to Listen to Sounds

To help you listen to the sounds of the Net, we have supplied a nice little freeware program called WPLAny; it's the creation of Bill Neisius. In conjunction with your PC's sound card, WPLAny can play sounds in WAV and VOC files, as well as sounds stored in three other formats. (For details, see Appendix B.)

WPLAny is free, which is attractive, and it's flexible, which is also attractive, but what really won us over is the fact that WPLAny is so elegantly designed. Once you've set up the appropriate associations in the File Manager, all you need to do is double-click on a sound file to listen to it. You don't have to pull down any menus, you don't have to click on any buttons, you don't have to interact with any funky Windows gadgets. In fact, WPLAny takes up *no screen space at all*. If, like us, you believe that sounds are meant to be heard and not seen, you'll appreciate WPLAny as much as we do.

## Installing WPLAny

WPLAny is distributed as a ZIP file, so you install it using WinZip in the usual manner:

1. **Create directories**: Create a new directory, *c:\wplany,* on your hard disk. This is where you'll install WPLAny. You may use a different directory for the installation, if you like, but in the instructions that follow, we assume you're going to install in *c:\wplany.* You'll also need a directory on your hard disk where you can store temporary files. We assume you'll use *c:\temp,* and you should create this directory if it does not already exist. Of course, you are free to use any directory you like for temporary files, but in the instructions that follow, we assume you'll use *c:\temp.*

2. **Extract files and create a Program Manager group**: From the *programs* directory of this book's diskette, copy *wplny09c.zip* into *c:\temp.* In the File Manager, double-click on *c:\temp-\wplny09c.zip* to run WinZip on it. In WinZip, click on **CheckOut** to bring up the CheckOut dialog box. Enter *c:\wplany* in the *Directory* box; the dialog box should look like this:

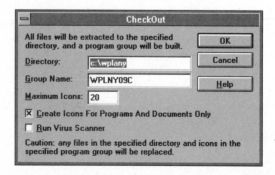

You could also check the *Run Virus Scanner* box, but *wplny09c.zip* was checked for viruses before being approved for distribution with this book, so you may wish, as shown here, to speed up the CheckOut process by omitting the virus-scanning step.

Click on **OK** to have WinZip extract the files from the archive and to create a new Program Manager group containing icons for WPLAny and its documentation. The new group will look much like this:

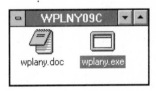

In the WinZip window, select **Close Archive** from the **File** menu, then click on **No** when you are presented with this window:

Exit WinZip.

3. **Set up File Manager associations**: Associate the following file extensions with *c:\wplany-\wplany.exe*: *.wav*, *.voc*, *.snd*, *.au*, and *.iff*. For instructions on setting up File Manager associations, see page 43.

4. **Delete an unnecessary file**: You no longer need the file *c:\temp\wplny09c.zip*, because it's just a copy of a file that's in the *programs* directory of this book's diskette. We recommend you delete *c:\temp\wplny09c.zip* to save disk space.

Voilà! WPLany is installed.

## Running WPLAny

It would be difficult to make WPLAny any easier to use. To listen to a sound file, double-click on it in the File Manager. WPLAny will automatically be launched, and you'll hear the contents of the file through your PC's speakers or headphones. If you get tired of listening to a sound file, double-click on it again, and WPLAny will stop playing it. What could be simpler than that?

As an example, double-click on *welcome.wav* in the *samples* directory of the diskette that comes with this book. When you do, you'll hear a greeting from one of the authors.

## For More Information

 WPLAny is a small program, so there's not a lot to say about it, but if you'd like to read what there is, take a look at the file *wplany.doc*. This is a simple text file, so you should read it using Notepad; there's no need to use a high-powered word processor like FrameMaker on it. You can also double-click on *wplany.exe* in the File Manager, in which case you will be presented with a window that provides some information about the program.

## Registering WPLAny

Rejoice! WPLAny is freeware, so you needn't worry about registration or a registration fee.

## Using Sound Recorder to Edit WAV Files

One of the programs that comes as a standard part of Windows 3.1 is the Sound Recorder, which you'll find in the Program Manager's **Accessories** group. This program only understands WAV files, but it's easy to use, and you can perform some interesting tricks with it. As a result, it's worth knowing how to use the Sound Recorder.

When you double-click on the Sound Recorder icon in the Program Manager, you're presented with this window:

The buttons along the bottom of the window perform functions analogous to those on a cassette player. From left to right, they let you rewind, fast forward, play, stop, and record a sound, though you'll need a microphone hooked up to your sound card if you want to record sounds.

The real power of the Sound Recorder, however, is accessed through its menus. Under the **Edit** menu, for instance, you'll find commands to mix sounds together, to insert one sound into another, and to remove portions of a sound. Commands under the **Effects** menu let you increase or decrease the volume or speed of a sound file, and they also give you the ability to add echo to a sound or to reverse a sound file so you can play it backwards.

To learn more about the capabilities of the Sound Recorder, consult your Windows documentation or click on the Sound Recorder's **Help** menu to peruse its online documentation.

# Movies and Your PC

OK, you've got pictures. You've got sounds. Now what about motion? You can do it — with digitization again, of course. You can now find digitized movies that are downloadable and playable on your personal computer.

Just like images and sounds, PC movies come in a variety of different file formats. On the Net, however, the most common format is that of MPEG, the Moving Photographic Experts Group. The MPEG format was designed by experts who were right down the hall from the JPEG gang; they even used JPEG technology in designing the MPEG format. MPEG files generally have the extension *.mpg*.

An alternative format is AVI (Audio Video Interleave), which is being pushed by Microsoft. Currently, it's of less importance to downloaders than the MPEG format, because very few files in AVI format are available for downloading. AVI files tend to have the extension *.avi*.

A third movie format is the Quicktime format. Quicktime is a movie player that runs on the Macintosh, but its counterpart in the PC world, Quicktime for Windows, reads the same movie files as the Mac program. Quicktime files usually have the extension *.mov*, and they, too, are a comparative rarity on the Net. For the time being, then, the only format you're likely to encounter when downloading movies is MPEG.

 Movies on the Net are usually short, sometimes only a few seconds long. They also tend to have small image sizes, often utilizing only a fraction of your screen. The primary reason for this is the size of movie files. They're big. They demand lots of disk space to store and lots of memory to show. For example, the movie supplied with this book uses only a portion of your monitor and lasts only about five seconds, yet it requires over 220,000 bytes of disk space. At that rate, a half-minute movie would demand well over a megabyte of disk space, and an hour-long movie would consume close to 160,000 *megabytes*!

 Most movies on the Net consist of video information along with a synchronized audio track (which comes in the form of a WAV file). If you have managed to resist getting a sound card until now, you'll have to run out and buy one if you want to appreciate the full range of movie magic. Without a sound card, you can still watch movies, but you'll miss out on the accompanying audio. Such silent movies may appeal to nostalgia buffs, but somehow it's just not the same. Of course, if you get a sound card, you'll also be able to enjoy the many sound files you can download from the Net.

## Using MPEGView to Watch Movies

Because most movies on the Net are in the form of MPEG files, you need a program that knows how to play movies in that format. It should not surprise you, then, to learn that we have included such a program with this book. In fact, we have included two programs, one for Windows and one for DOS. Neither requires a registration fee.

The package containing these movie-playing programs is called MPEGView, and it's the creation of Xing Technology Corporation. MPEGView's Windows program features a nice graphical interface that gives you full control over playing a movie, including the ability to step through it frame by frame. MPEGView's DOS program offers fewer features, but, as we describe later, it will sometimes do when the Windows program will not. Both programs suffer from the drawback that they fail to properly display some types of MPEG files. This drawback is not crippling, however, because MPEGView correctly displays most MPEG files that are currently available on the Net.

In the sections that follow, we show you how to install and run the MPEGView programs. After that, you're on your own to explore the exciting world of PC movies.

## Installing MPEGView

Like most downloadable software, MPEGView is distributed as a ZIP file, so you install it using WinZip:

1. **Create directories**: Create a new directory, *c:\mpegview,* on your hard disk. This is where you'll install MPEGView. You may use a different directory for the installation, but in the instructions that follow, we assume you'll use *c:\mpegview*. You will also need a directory on your hard disk where you can store temporary files. We assume you'll use *c:\temp*, and you should create this directory if it does not exist. Of course, you are free to use any directory you like for temporary files, but in the instructions that follow, we assume you'll use *c:\temp*.

2. **Extract files and create a Program Manager group**: From the *programs* directory of this book's diskette, copy *mpegvu.zip* into *c:\temp*. In the File Manager, double-click on *c:\temp\mpegvu.zip* to run WinZip on it. In WinZip, click on **CheckOut** to bring up the CheckOut dialog box. Enter *c:\mpegview* in the *Directory* box; the dialog box should look like this:

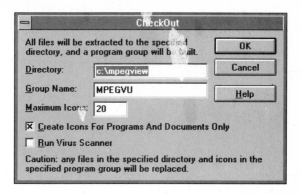

You could also have WinZip scan the files in *mpegvu.zip* for viruses, but that was done before the ZIP file was approved for distribution with this book, so you may want to speed up the extraction process by skipping that step.

Click on **OK** to have WinZip extract the files from the archive and to create a new Program Manager group containing icons for MPEGView and its documentation. The new group will look something like this:

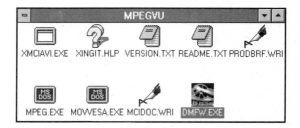

In the WinZip window, select **Close Archive** from the **File** menu, then click on **No** when you are presented with this window:

Exit WinZip.

3.  **Set up a File Manager association**: Associate the file extension *.mpg* with *c:\mpeg-view\dmfw.exe.* For a review of how to set up File Manager associations, see page 43.

4.  **Delete the unnecessary file**: You no longer need the file *c:\temp\mpegvu.zip*, because it's just a copy of a file that's in the *programs* directory of this book's diskette. We recommend you delete *c:\temp\mpegvu.zip* to save disk space.

You're now ready to dim the lights and settle into a comfortable chair, because MPEGView is installed.

## Running MPEGView

Running MPEGView is about as easy as it gets. To watch a movie, just use the File Manager to double-click on an *.mpg* file. When you do, MPEGView will open a window and play the movie for you; then the window will go away. It's that simple.

There is, however, one slight complication. When MPEGView plays a movie for the first time, it creates a small file in the same directory as the movie file. The contents of this new file are unimportant (it helps MPEGView show the movie), but MPEGView will insist on trying to create it. Therefore, you shouldn't try to view a movie unless MPEGView can create a file in the same directory as the movie.

As an example, there is a movie called *eggclock.mpg* in the *samples* directory of the diskette that comes with this book. If you double-click on this *.mpg* file in the File Manager, MPEGView will try to create a new file on the book's diskette. This attempt will fail, however, because the diskette comes write-protected so you can't accidentally modify the programs and sample files that are on it.

You can still view *eggclock.mpg*, of course, but first you have to copy it into a directory where MPEGView can create a new file. A reasonable place to copy it is into the directory you use for temporary files, usually *c:\temp*. Once you've done that, you can use the File Manager to double-click on *c:\temp\eggclock.mpg*, and the movie will start right up. When it does, it will initially look like this:

As you watch the movie, you'll see the egg get hit by a speeding projectile. The egg will explode from the impact, then it will turn into a clock with rapidly cycling hands. All the while, you'll hear the sound of an engine revving, then a vehicle screeching off at high speed. What all this means we're not sure, but it's certainly an interesting experience.

Another way to launch MPEGView is to invoke it directly, either by double-clicking on its icon in the Program Manager or by double-clicking on *c:\mpegview\dmfw.exe* in the File Manager. When you launch MPEGView this way, you'll see two things: a control panel and a movie window. Because you haven't specified a movie to watch yet, the movie window shows the logo for Xing Technology, the company that distributes MPEGView:

The buttons on the control panel allow you to play, stop, resize, and otherwise manhandle whatever movie you have loaded into MPEGView:

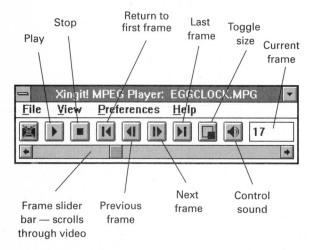

To load a movie, just choose **Open...** from the **File** menu, then use the resulting dialog box to specify the name of the *.mpg* file you'd like to see. When you do, MPEGView will display the initial frame of the movie. For example, if you load *eggclock.mpg*, the movie window will look exactly like the picture on page 125.

Once you have the first frame of a movie displayed, you can use the control panel to start the movie, stop it, restart it, move to the first or last frame of the movie, increase or decrease the picture size, and adjust the volume of the sound track.

## Other MPEGView Capabilities

After you have mastered the art of simply playing movies with MPEGView, you will want to explore some of its more advanced capabilities. Here are a few things you can do:

- **Cycle through one or more movies continuously**: Use the **Open...** command under the **File** menu to open one or more MPEG files. Use the **File** menu twice more to turn on **Cycle** and **Repeat**. Then sit back and watch them go! When you get tired of the non-stop entertainment, click on the control panel's **Stop** button.

- **Go to a specific frame**: You can display the movie frame of your choice. Just double-click on the frame number to highlight it, then type a number. The frame you specify will immediately be made the current frame. You can also use the slider buttons to increase and decrease the current frame number one frame at a time.

- **Save a frame in a file**: You can save an individual movie frame as a *.bmp* file, which can then be imported into a document, used as wallpaper for your Windows desktop, or edited with a program like LView Pro.

To save a frame of a movie, load the movie into MPEGView, then go to the frame you want to save. Select **Save Frame as...** from the **File** menu, then click on **8 Bit**. (You could click on **24 Bit** instead, but unless you are using a monitor that can display millions of colors at a time, saving a 24-bit image isn't worth your trouble — or your disk space.) Use the resulting dialog box to specify the name of the file in which you'd like to store the image. Then click on **OK**.

As an example, this is frame 10 of *eggclock.mpg*:

## Running MPEGView in DOS

Some PCs don't have the power it takes to produce acceptable movie playback in Windows. If this is the case for you, try the DOS version of the program, which requires less memory and can get by with a slower processor.

The DOS program is called *mpeg.exe*, and it's one of the files included in the MPEGView archive. To view a movie from DOS, just type **mpeg** and the name of the movie file you'd like to see. For example, to watch *eggclock.mpg* from DOS, just type this:

```
mpeg eggclock.mpg
```

(If you'd like to be able to do this from any DOS directory on your computer, you'll have to make sure that *mpeg.exe* is on your DOS path. If you don't know what your DOS path is, or if you're not sure how to add a file like *mpeg.exe* to your path, consult your DOS documentation or give the command

```
help path
```

to access DOS's online documentation.)

The DOS version of MPEGView is less powerful than the Windows version. The only thing you can do with it is play movie files. You can't stop, pause, back up, or do any of the other nifty tricks available in the Windows version. For that reason, you should try to run the Windows program if you possibly can. Of course, you're already a Windows user, so we need hardly remind you that doing things in Windows is usually superior to doing them in DOS.

## For More Information

MPEGView comes with several documentation files, including the ever-popular *readme.txt*; that's always a good place to start. You can also read MPEGView's online documentation, which you can access in the conventional ways: either double-click on *c:\mpegview\xingit.hlp* in the File Manager, or click on the **Help** menu item when running the Windows version of MPEGView.

## Registration Information

MPEGView is free, but it's a form of crippleware that might more appropriately be called "demoware."

Xing Technology Corporation uses MPEGView to bring their line of MPEG-related products to your attention. However, MPEGView doesn't offer all the features that Xing's commercial products do. In particular, MPEG-View won't let you edit movie files, nor will it play every file that is in the MPEG format.

If you'd like to find out how to purchase a product that will lift these restrictions, you should get in touch with Xing Technology. You'll find contact information in several of the files that come with MPEGView. Look, for example, at *readme.txt* and *prodbrf.wri*. If you'd prefer to get your information while running the program, click on **File**, then on **About...**, and you'll be presented with Xing Technology's telephone numbers.

# 7

# Resources
# for
# Downloaders

Let's face it, going online has become more than fun, it's become *trendy*, and where trends are found, charlatans are sure to be lurking nearby. The result has been a veritable cavalcade of books on networks, networking, the Internet, and — with the notable exception of downloading — all other things Net-related. Unfortunately, of the bevy of books we've managed to plow through, most leave us less than thrilled. Some are inaccurate, many are incomplete, most are confusing, and nearly all are just plain poorly written. Such is the price of trendiness.

Of course, we haven't read all the available books. Please — we have lives. Still, we've read enough to know that the odds of randomly picking a good one are not in your favor. At the same time, we have no illusions that *The Downloader's Companion*, inspired literary masterpiece though it may be, contains the answers to all your questions. To aid you in your quest for a higher level of technical enlightenment, then, we present the following selective list of recommended books, books that stand apart from the masses as uniquely informative, uncommonly well-written, and, in many cases, just plain fun to read.

We've divided our discussion into five categories. The first is devoted to books that discuss going and being online in general terms, i.e., without making any assumptions about the online services you use or the parts of the Net you connect to. The second category concerns itself with books on commercial online services. It contains only a single entry, but that one's a goodie, and we think you'll like it. We then take up the almost limitless topic of the Internet, and we recommend not only conventional books, we also point you to books on the Internet you can download from the Internet itself! Our last two categories of books are aimed at those of you who would like to know more about the details, technical and otherwise, of archiving, data compression, and representation formats for images and sounds.

Once we've dispensed with the books, we move on to a higher-tech topic: CD-ROMs. In particular, we discuss CD-ROMs that contain copies of the software available from two of the the best-known and most useful Internet repositories. Such repositories contain thousands of freeware and shareware programs, so CD-ROMs that duplicate their contents are well worth knowing about.

## Books about Going and Being Online

The contenders are legion, but the only text we've seen that can legitimately claim to be truly *encyclopedic* about being online is this appropriately entitled book:

*The Online User's Encyclopedia*, by Bernard
Aboba, Addison-Wesley, Reading, Massachusetts,
1993,   ISBN 0-201-62214-9. 803 pages.

Aboba's book covers nearly everything you'd ever
want to know about going online, being online, all but
*living* online. It discusses bulletin boards, the Internet,
and commercial online services like Compuserve, Prodigy, GEnie, and America Online; it describes modems
and the astonishingly obscure commands needed to
control them; it describes the differences between
UUCP, USENET, BITNET, RIME, and other acronyms;
it identifies likely places on the Internet to look for files
and discussions on a wide variety of topics; it repro-
duces essays on the history of various networks; and it
has eleven (eleven!) appendices — a full 200 pages —
summarizing recommended products (both hardware
and software), how to communicate with Unix (should
you find yourself in the unfortunate position of having
to do so), even an extensive glossary. Of course, it's not
perfect. Aboba's writing could use some improvement,
his treatment of many topics is somewhat superficial
(for example, downloading), and sometimes he uses
terms before he defines them (if he defines them at all),
but such matters pale in comparison to the enormous
amount of information the book provides. Our summary of file extensions in Appendices A and B draws
heavily on information in Aboba's book.

If you're interested in what's available online in the way
of newsgroups, mailing lists, and file repositories, the
best general-purpose resource we know of is

*NETGUIDE: Your Map to the Services, Informa-
tion and Entertainment on the Electronic High-
way*, Random House Electronic Publishing, New
York, 1994, ISBN 0-679-75106-8. 356 pages.

Modeled after *TV Guide*, the unique strength of this
entertaining book is its coverage of virtually every online
service, including the Internet, CompuServe, Prodigy,
America Online, and GEnie, as well as several hundred

BBS systems. So if you want to know where to go for, say, all the information on Star Trek you can possibly stomach, this book will tell you, regardless of which part of the information superhighway you happen to be cruising. This is especially valuable for finding out about specialty BBS systems, because they are usually much less well publicized than the national and international networks with which they compete (or at least coexist).

The book is organized by topic, something like the yellow pages in a telephone book, but it also contains an index that should help you find just what you're looking for. The only shortcoming of *NETGUIDE* is that it's not particularly comprehensive. Only so much information fits into 356 pages, and that's not enough space to do justice to the forums on CompuServe or the newsgroups on the Internet, much less all of both, plus all the resources of the other networks and BBS systems. Still, you wouldn't want to lug around a definitive 25,000-page tome (which would be out of date by the time it was published, by the way, so rapidly are things expanding out in Netland), and you will enjoy perusing *NETGUIDE*, so we recommend you give it a try.

## Books about Commercial Online Services

Books dedicated to describing particular online services are multiplying like rabbits, but if you're looking for something a little more general, especially something that can help you assess the strengths and weaknesses of the three largest commercial services (Prodigy, CompuServe, and America Online), the book for you is

*Cruising Online: Larry Magid's Guide To The New Digital Highways*, by Lawrence J. Magid, Random House Electronic Publishing, New York, 1994, ISBN 0-679-75155-6. 481 pages.

Magid is a professional writer, and it shows: his prose is easy to digest, and his explanations are lucid. Furthermore (and unlike most other books on the Net), he includes a lot of pictures of what your screen will look like when you do certain things, so you can confirm that the computer is behaving the way you're supposed to expect it to.

In view of the fact that *Cruising Online* covers three services (plus an overview chapter on the Internet), it is remarkably comprehensive. It contains material on the cost of each service, how to get connected, how to send and receive electronic mail, how to join discussion groups, how to shop, how to get news and weather reports, how to get business and financial data, how to consult encyclopedias and other reference works, even how to download files. Of course, books specializing in one service or another contain information not found in Magid's guide, but for a useful introduction to the three big commercial networks, this book is tough to beat.

## Books about The Internet

 In many ways, the Internet is undergoing the most rapid growth and change of any of the online information networks, and most authors must struggle with the fact that their books are certain to be out of date by the time they arrive on the shelves. It is noteworthy, then, that our favorite Internet book is a newly revised edition of one of the first to come out on the topic. Originally published in 1992, the first edition is a classic that has held its value, and the second edition is everything the first one was, only more so.

*The Whole Internet User's Guide & Catalog,* Second Edition, by Ed Krol, O'Reilly & Associates, Inc., Sebastopol, California, 1994, ISBN 1-56592-063-5. 543 pages.

What's really nice about Krol's book is how he achieves a balance between explaining the commands you need to understand to get around the Internet (commands like ftp, rlogin, telnet, mail, rn, archie, gopher, wais, mosaic, etc.) and describing the resources available on the Internet and where you can find them. Just as the title says, it truly is both a User's Guide and a Catalog.

Krol's book is also noteworthy for its refined look. No super-fancy neon-colored graphics on the cover, no overly-hyped high-tech look. Just a beautiful, readable layout and typesetting that results in a book that is both informative and easy to use. Our only complaint is that the index isn't as comprehensive as it could be. Still, we like *The Whole Internet User's Guide* a lot, and we think you will, too.

For a more eclectic view of the Internet, turn to the Internet itself and download an entire book of useful information! (You thought you could only download programs, images, and sounds? Shame on you — you underestimate the power of the Net!) In particular, download

*EFF's Guide To The Internet*, by Adam Gaffin with Jörg Heitkötter, 1993 (but updated on a regular basis). Available in a variety of formats via anonymous ftp from ftp.eff.org.

This book was originally called *The Big Dummy's Guide to the Internet*, and we were a bit saddened to see the demise of such a catchy title, but the mainstream name doesn't detract from what is fundamentally a wild ride through Internetland. The book doesn't exhibit the careful attention to detail displayed by Krol's book, but it does a much better job of conveying the attitude of joyous abandon that so frequently characterizes Internet inhabitants. In addition to providing perfectly adequate coverage of the expected topics — how to get connected, electronic mail, newsgroups, telnet, archie, ftp, gopher, wais, worldwide web, and the other usual suspects — it finds time to delve into such esoterica as how to get the *exact* time by querying an atomic clock run by the U.S. Government in Boulder, Colorado. (By the way, there are several shareware programs floating around that synchronize your PC's clock with that of the U.S. Naval Observatory; look for them on the Net.)

Don't be fooled by the fact that *EFF's Guide* can be downloaded for free: it's as professionally put together as any book you'll find in your local bookstore, and the fact that it's electronically updated on a regular basis means the information it contains is likely to be much more current than even the newest hardcopy books you can find.

That notwithstanding, *EFF's Guide* should be available as a "real" book by the end of 1994, although in that form it will have yet another title, this time *Everybody's Guide to the Internet*. Its existence in both downloadable and bound form will put it in the company of another Internet classic, *Zen and the Art of the Internet*. (To find the online version of that book, use your Internet service's search capability to look for files on the Net whose names contain "zen".) For having something to read on a beach or carry on a plane, a bound book can't be beat, but for searching, editing, electronically updating, and otherwise manipulating the information in a book, an electronic copy of the text is without equal.

Other books on the Internet you can download include *The Hitchhiker's Guide to the Internet* (search for files with "hhgi" in the name) and *Surfing the Internet* (try searching for files with "surf" in the name, and don't be surprised if you get a lot of hits on things that have little to do with information superhighways and much to do with riding waves).

If you're going to be wallowing in the boundless resources of the Internet (which we highly recommend), you'll find *NETGUIDE*'s coverage of what's available a bit too scant. A useful supplement is

*The Internet Yellow Pages*, by Harley Hahn and Rick Stout, Osborne McGraw-Hill, Berkeley, California, 1994, ISBN 0-07-882023-5. 447 pages.

In typical anarchic Internet fashion, there are two different books calling themselves the *Internet Yellow Pages*, but don't be fooled — this is the one you want. It's not totally comprehensive, but nothing on the Internet ever is, and Hahn and Stout have done a good job of listing the topics that are most likely to interest you in a fun, readable, interesting format. Just perusing the topics is entertaining. Where else are you going to find out how to locate the racy pictures you've heard so much about, how to look up the lyrics of your favorite songs, and how to send electronic mail to celebrities ranging from the President of the United States to Beavis and Butt-head? The book ends with a nice listing of all Usenet newsgroups (that is of necessity out of date long before the ink ever hits the paper) and a very usable index. In spite of the fact that Hahn and Stout take every opportunity to push their other Internet book (a book that did *not* meet our stringent criteria for inclusion in this chapter), we say check this one out.

## Books about Archiving and Compression

Our treatment of file archives and data compression has been fairly superficial, focusing almost entirely on the process of extracting files from archives and uncompressing them for use. From a pragmatic point of view, this is pretty much all that you, as a downloader, will ever have occasion to do. Archiving and compression programs are much more powerful than this, however, and you may well want to take advantage of their additional capabilities some day, either because you'd like to make better use of your computer's disk space or because you'd like to create archives of your own to be *uploaded* to the Net for others to download and enjoy.

A good place to learn more about archiving and compression programs is this book:

*PKZip, LHARC & Co.: The Ultimate Data Compression Book*, by Irene Kespret, Abacus Books, Grand Rapids, Michigan, 1993, ISBN 1-55755-203-7. 243 pages, one diskette of software included.

Kespret describes, in general terms, the theory on which data compression programs are based and explains why different kinds of files require different approaches to data compression. She provides a lot of information on how to compress files and create archives using several common programs, and the book concludes with an extensive summary of the commands available for these programs: ARJ 2.30, LHA 2.13, PKZip/PKUNZIP, and ZOO. If you're looking for specific information on how to use other compression programs (e.g., the Unix compress program), you'll have to look elsewhere.

It's hard to argue with the software that Kespret chose to bundle with her book, because much of it is the same as the archiving and compression software we've included with this book. Of course, Kespret's narrower focus means that she fails to offer the goodies for decoding files, displaying images, and playing movies and sounds that we've thoughtfully provided for you. In addition, the software that comes with *The Downloader's Companion* tends to be more recent than that accompanying Kespret's book.

We've tried very hard to shield you from the minutiae of archiving, data compression, representation formats for images and sounds, etc., but the thought has occurred to us that you might actually *want* to know some of the details we've deliberately omitted. Not to worry. If you'd like a broader discussion of data compression that includes these topics, you are familiar with the C programming language, and you aren't put off by sentences like "Using QIC-122 encoding, this will take exactly sixteen bits to encode, which means it encodes 8 bytes of data with only 2 bytes," we can recommend

*The Data Compression Book*, by Mark Nelson, M&T Books, New York, NY, 1992, ISBN 1-55851-216-0. 527 pages, two diskettes of software included.

Given the book's highly technical content, Nelson's prose is actually quite palatable, and if his general explanations of data compression don't answer all your questions, his C programs that implement the algorithms certainly will. The book covers general data compression in the tradition of programs like PKZip and ARJ, as well as specialized compression techniques for speech and graphics.

The book's treatment of sound representation is interesting, but its failure to specifically examine WAV files is disappointing. Similarly, Nelson's treatment of GIF and MPEG files is all but nonexistent, but this is compensated for somewhat by his explanation of the JPEG standard in all its mathematical glory.

## Books about Graphics and Sounds

There aren't many books available that discuss representation formats for images and sounds, and those few that do exist tend to be aimed at the technically hard-core. However, we've found a couple of gems that do an excellent job of explaining things for non-experts. For information on representing images and other graphics on a PC, consider this:

*Graphics File Formats*, David C. Kay and John R. Levine, Windcrest/McGraw-Hill, 1992, ISBN 0-8306-3059-7. 278 pages.

Kay's and Levine's book is a handy guide to the frighteningly large number of graphics formats that are in use on PCs. Oddly enough, JPEG is not among the formats listed on the back of the book as being covered, but fear not: it, too, is described in the text. Perhaps the best feature of the book is its concise and intelligible summaries of the advantages and disadvantages of each graphics format it discusses. That there are 23 such formats (excluding those in the "Other Formats" chapter) gives you some idea of the current state of standardization facing the field of PC graphics. (You know what they say: the nice thing about standards is that there are so many to choose from.) Be glad you're on the viewing end of things instead of the programming end.

The introduction begins by clearing up the mysteries of how a photograph becomes a digitized image, the methods for representing images digitally, how computers deal with color and greyscale, and how images are compressed. It goes on to describe all 23 different graphics formats, including GIF and JPEG. The language is simple, straightforward, and concise. This book is packed with information that will be useful to both the neophyte and the experienced graphics person needing a reference on graphics file formats.

For the aurally inclined, we suggest

*Welcome to... PC Sound, Music and MIDI*, by Tom Benford, MIS Press, 1993, ISBN 1-55828-316-1. 306 pages, one CD-ROM with music, sounds, and software included.

*The Downloader's Companion*, useful and informative as it is, has given you just a taste of sounds and sound files; *Welcome to... PC Sound, Music and MIDI* provides the entire meal by dishing up a well-written introduction into the world of sound, sampling, MIDI recording, and the hardware and software that make it happen. The book is intended to take the beginning music lover to an intermediate state of digital bliss. It covers all the topics you'll want to know if you are getting into digital recording, including reviews of software, musical equipment, voice and speech recognition, and a list of computer games with great sounds. Interestingly, it also contains interviews (in both written and audio form) with a number of artists who are movers and shakers in the field of electronic instruments, MIDI, and PC-based music synthesis.

We found the book particularly useful, because it not only explains how analog sounds become digitized signals, it also describes sound file formats, their pros and cons, and how they are best used. It also contains a glossary that defines dozens of terms commonly used in the PC music and recording biz.

The CD-ROM that comes with the book contains both conventional sound tracks (so you can listen to them) as well as a grab-bag of programs and other files. Inexplicably, the book contains no description of the files and software on the CD, nor does the CD itself contain a file describing its contents. As a result, you have to hunt around a good bit to figure out exactly what's available. For example, the CD contains both MID (see page 151) and WAV files for selected portions of *The Nutcracker Suite* (very convenient for putting your PC in the Christmas spirit), but we were a bit surprised to find them in the directory *nautilus*. Nautilus? Go figure.

## *CD-ROMs of Internet Repositories*

So you break into a cold sweat at the very thought of all that software — *terabytes* of software (that's thousands of megabytes) — sitting on the Internet, ripe for the picking. But you don't have or can't afford access to the Internet. Or you have access, but your modem is ancient, and you've got better things to do than crawl along the Information Autobahn at 2400 baud or less. Or you're tired of constantly logging in to the Internet, ftp-ing to one software repository or another, grabbing some files, then waiting for them to download. What you really want is fast, easy, *direct* access to the files you know are available and that you're dying to get your greedy little hands on. If your computer has a CD-ROM drive, there is a way.

 There are now companies whose business consists of making copies of the most popular software repositories on the Net and selling them as CDs. Such companies offer dozens of titles, but the ones of primary interest to Windows users are those containing copies of the justly famous Internet CICA and SIMTEL repositories.

It is hard to imagine the diversity of software contained on these CDs. Simply put, if you want a program to do something, you can almost certainly find one here. Often, you will find more than one. That's the good news. The bad news is twofold. First, the contents of the CICA and SIMTEL repositories are constantly changing, so by the time a CD is printed, it's already somewhat out of date. To help you combat this problem, some companies will sell you a subscription to the CDs: a few times each year (usually quarterly) they'll ship you a new CD containing the latest contents of the repository to which you've subscribed.

The second problem is that the repositories themselves are not particularly well indexed, so you have to poke around quite a bit to find out what's available. Given a CD with over 600 megabytes of software, that's a lot of poking. If you think of it as looking for the proverbial needle in a proverbial haystack covering several square proverbial miles, you may begin to get an idea of what sifting through these repositories can be like. Still, the CICA and SIMTEL repositories constitute an invaluable resource for Windows users, so you should seriously consider checking them out.

As we write this in the summer of 1994, we're aware of two companies that sell CD-ROMs of the CICA and SIMTEL repositories. They are:

Walnut Creek CDROM          Voice: 800/786-9907
1547 Palos Verdes           Voice: 510/674-0783
Suite 260                   Fax:   510/674-0821
Walnut Creek, CA 94596      Email: info@cdrom.com
USA

InfoMagic, Inc.             Voice: 800/800-6613
PO Box 30370                Voice: 602/526-9565
Flagstaff, AZ 86003         Fax:   602/526-9573
USA                         Email: info@infomagic.com

Of course, it's important to remember that these CDs merely reproduce what is already freely available on the Internet, so if you *do* have Internet access, you may wish to copy files straight from CICA and SIMTEL. The CICA repository is at ftp.cica.indiana.edu in the directory */pub/ pc/win3*. The SIMTEL repository is mirrored at many sites, including wuarchive.wustl.edu in the directory */systems/ibmpc*. (If the last two sentences make no sense to you, consult a good book on the Internet. We recommend *The Whole Internet User's Guide & Catalog* — see page 135).

# Net File Extensions (Alphabetical)

In this appendix and the one that follows, we summarize the most common meanings of a multitude of extensions you may stumble across as you roam the Netscape. This appendix is organized alphabetically by extension. Appendix B presents the same information, but it organizes extensions by category. So if you're faced with a file with a particular extension and you'd like to know what that file is likely to contain, this is the place to come. On the other hand, if you want to know the common extensions for a particular kind of file (e.g., graphics files or file archives, etc.), look in Appendix B.

Some extensions indicate files that are designed for use on other kinds of computers, most notably Macintoshes and computers running the Unix operating system. Because Unix is case-sensitive, users of that system distinguish between upper- and lower-case letters. As a result, there is a difference between the extension *.z* (lower-case z) and *.Z* (upper-case Z). In the table that follows, all extensions are listed in lower case unless Unix explicitly expects an extension to use upper-case letters.

Extensions corresponding to files you can manipulate using the software provided with this book are listed in boldface. (Notice that there are many of them. This is a very good book. You were wise to purchase it.) Extensions corresponding to files you can manipulate using software that comes standard with Windows are italicized.

If you don't have the software to manipulate files in a particular format, look first to the Net to see if you can download the necessary programs. In many cases, you'll not only be able to do it, you'll have no choice, because the requisite programs are often unavailable except through freeware or shareware.

Finally, keep in mind that there are no official standards for what file extensions are supposed to mean, just conventions followed by most members of the Net community. As a result, if you see a file that ends in *.zip*, there's a very good chance it's an archive produced by PKZip or a compatible program (e.g., WinZip), but there's no guarantee it doesn't contain something completely different. This can be frustrating at times, but it's also part of the fun; there's something to be said for a little anarchy.

Much of the information that follows is based on tables in Bernard Aboba's *Online User's Encyclopedia*, which is described in Chapter 7 of this book.

*.1st*    Usually used as the extension of a documentation file you should read immediately after extracting the contents of an archive, e.g., *readme.1st*. Use Notepad to view or edit the file.

.ai       A graphic produced by Adobe Illustrator.

.arc      A compressed archive produced by ARC. Use WinZip in conjunction with one of the DOS programs that reads ARC archives to extract the files. (Such programs are described in

Chapter 4.) To add files to ARC archives, you'll need a copy of the ARC program. If you use the File Manager to associate WinZip with *.arc* files, you'll be able to run WinZip on those archives by double-clicking on them.

**.arj** A compressed archive produced by ARJ. Use WinZip or ARJ to extract the files or otherwise manipulate the archive. If you use the File Manager to associate WinZip with *.arj* files, you'll be able to run WinZip on those archives by double-clicking on them.

*.asc* A text file in ASCII format. Use Notepad to view or edit the file.

**.au** A sound file for Sun, DEC, and NExT workstations. Use WPLAny to listen to it. If you use the File Manager to associate WPLAny with *.au* files, you'll be able to listen to them by double-clicking on them.

.avi A movie in Video for Windows format. If you have the appropriate MCI device driver installed, you can double-click on the file to run Windows' Media Player on it.

*.bat* A DOS batch file. This is an executable file, but it's also textual, so you can use Notepad to view or edit it. To run the file, double-click on it.

.bin A binary file. Such files are almost never portable from one kind of computer to another.

.bit A monochrome bitmap from a PC.

**.bmp** A color bitmap for Windows or OS/2. Use LView Pro to view or edit it. If you use the File Manager to associate LView Pro with *.bmp* files, you'll be able to run LView Pro on those files by double-clicking on them.

.c        A program written in the C programming language.

.C        A program written in the C++ programming language. This extension is primarily used under Unix.

.cc       A program written in the C++ programming language.

.cdr      A graphic produced by Corel Draw.

.cgm      A graphics metafile.

*.com*     An executable DOS file. To run the file, double-click on it.

.cpp      A program written in the C++ programming language.

.cpt      An archive produced by Compact Pro. Primarily used on the Mac.

.csv      A spreadsheet represented as comma-separated values.

.cxx      A program written in the C++ programming language.

.cmu      A graphic produced by the Unix-based CMU Window Manager.

.dbf      A file produced by dBASE.

.dd       A compressed archive produced by Disk Doubler; used on the Mac.

.dll      A Windows dynamically linked library file.

.doc   In the context of Windows, this usually indicates a document created with Microsoft Word, but it can also indicate a document created with FrameMaker.

*.doc*   In the context of DOS or Unix, this usually indicates a text file, typically documentation for an accompanying program. Use Notepad to view or edit the file.

.dox   A document produced by MultiMate.

.drw   A graphic produced by either Macdraw or Micrographx Draw. To make things interesting, the two programs write their files in different formats.

.dvi   A "device-independent" version of a document that's been prepared for printing in general, but has not yet been prepared for a particular printer. Produced by the TeX typesetting system. Primarily used under Unix.

.dxf   A graphic produced by AutoCAD.

.eps   A graphic in encapsulated PostScript format.

.epsf   A graphic in encapsulated PostScript format.

*.exe*   An executable file, typically a program, but sometimes a self-extracting archive. To run the file, double-click on it.

.fax   As Bernard Aboba puts it in his *Online User's Encyclopedia*, this indicates a file in "one of dozens of incompatible fax formats."

**.gif**   An image in GIF format. Use LView Pro to view or edit it. If you use the File Manager to associate LView Pro with *.gif* files, you'll be able to run LView Pro on those files by double-clicking on them.

.gz       A compressed archive in GNU Zip format. Primarily used under Unix. Don't be fooled by the similar names: files in this format are not compatible with programs like WinZip that know how to process standard *.zip* files.

.h        A header file for a program written in the C or C++ programming languages.

*.hlp*    If designed for Windows, a Windows help file. Double-click on the file to start the help system on it. If not designed for Windows (e.g., if designed for DOS), often a text file you can read with Notepad.

.hpk      A compressed archive produced by HPack.

.hpgl     A file prepared for plotting on an HP plotter.

.hqx      An archive produced by BinHex. Primarily used on the Mac.

.html     A document in the hypertext markup language. Used by the World-Wide Web, a tool for accessing information on the Internet.

**.iff**  A sound file for the Amiga. Use WPLAny to listen to it. If you use the File Manager to associate WPLAny with *.iff* files, you'll be able to listen to them by double-clicking on them.

.image    A file containing an exact binary image of a Macintosh disk.

.img      A graphic produced by GEM Paint.

**.jpg**  An image in JPEG format. Use LView Pro to view or edit it. If you use the File Manager to associate LView Pro with *.jpg* files, you'll be able to run LView Pro on those files by double-clicking on them.

.lbm    A graphic produced by Deluxe Paint.

*.lst*    A textual listing of some type. Use Notepad to view or edit the file.

**.lzh**    A compressed archive produced by LHA. Use WinZip or LHA to extract the files or otherwise manipulate the archive. If you use the File Manager to associate WinZip with *.lzh* files, you'll be able to run WinZip on those archives by double-clicking on them.

.mac    A bitmap format for the Mac.

*.me*    Usually used as the extension of a README file, i.e., *read.me*. Use Notepad to view or edit the file.

.mid    A MIDI sound file. If you have the appropriate MCI device driver installed, you can double-click on the file to run Windows' Media Player on it.

**.mme**    A MIME-encoded file. Use XferPro to decode it. If you use the File Manager to associate Xfer-Pro with *.mme* files, you'll be able to run Xfer-Pro on those files by double-clicking on them.

**.mpg**    A movie in MPEG format. Use the MPEGView program DMFW to view it. If you use the File Manager to associate DMFW with *.mpg* files, you'll be able to watch them by double-clicking on them. If DMFW provides unsatisfactory performance, you may wish to view MPEG movies under DOS; see Chapter 6 for details on how to do it.

.msp   A graphic. Double-click on the file to run Paintbrush on it.

.pak   A compressed archive produced by Pak.

.pbm   A graphical bitmap in Portable Bitmap format. Used primarily under Unix.

.pcl   A file prepared for printing on an HP Laserjet printer.

.pcc   A graphic. Use Paintbrush to view or edit it.

.pcx   A graphic. Double-click on the file to run Paintbrush on it.

.pgm   A greyscale graphic produced by PBMPLUS.

.pic   A graphic produced by Lotus 1-2-3, Paul Mace Pictor, or Grasp.

.pit   An archive produced by PackIt. Primarily used on the Mac.

.ppm   A color graphic produced by PBMPLUS.

.ps    A document or image in PostScript format, which is designed for printers. Primarily used under Unix. You'll need a PostScript previewer (available for free downloading from the Internet—look for a program called Ghostscript) or a PostScript printer to see the document or the image.

.ras   A raster image format for Sun workstations.

.rle   A graphic format for raster images.

.rtf   A document in Rich Text Format. Some word processors (e.g., Microsoft Word, FrameMaker) can display these files correctly.

.sea    A self-extracting archive for the Mac.

.sgml   A document in Standard Generalized Markup Language (SGML). This format is an emerging standard, and it is likely that full-featured word processors will eventually be able to read such files and display them correctly.

.shar   A textual archive produced by shar. Used primarily under Unix.

.sit    An archive produced by StuffIt; primarily used on the Mac.

**.snd**   A sound file for Sounder/Soundtools. Use WPLAny to listen to it. If you use the File Manager to associate WPLAny with *.snd* files, you'll be able to listen to them by double-clicking on them.

.snd   A sound file for the Macintosh.

.sqz   A compressed archive produced by Squeeze.

.syl   A spreadsheet in Microsoft SYLK format.

.tar   An archive produced by tar. Primarily used under Unix.

.tex   A document written using TeX typesetting commands. You'll need the TeX software (available for free downloading from the Internet— look for CTAN, the Comprehensive TeX Archive Network) to produce the formatted document.

**.tga**   An image in TrueVision Targa format. Use LView Pro to view or edit it. If you use the File Manager to associate LView Pro with *.tga* files, you'll be able to run LView Pro on those files by double-clicking on them.

.tif    A graphic in TIFF format.

.tiff   A graphic in TIFF format.

*.txt*  A text file. Use Notepad to view or edit it.

**.uu**   A uuencoded file. Use XferPro to decode it. If you use the File Manager to associate XferPro with *.uu* files, you'll be able to run XferPro on those files by double-clicking on them.

**.uue**  A uuencoded file. Use XferPro to decode it. If you use the File Manager to associate XferPro with *.uue* files, you'll be able to run XferPro on those files by double-clicking on them.

**.voc**  A sound file for DOS. Use WPLAny to listen to it. If you use the File Manager to associate WPLAny with *.voc* files, you'll be able to listen to them by double-clicking on them.

.w51    A document produced by WordPerfect 5.1.

**.*wav***  A sound file for Windows. Use WPLAny to listen to it. If you use the File Manager to associate WPLAny with *.wav* files, you'll be able to listen to them by double-clicking on them. You can use the Sound Recorder that comes with Windows to edit *.wav* files; see Chapter 6 for information on how to do it.

.wk1    A spreadsheet in Lotus 1-2-3 format.

.wk2    A spreadsheet in Lotus 1-2-3 format.

.wk3    A spreadsheet in Lotus 1-2-3 format.

.win    A graphic produced by TrueVision Targa.

.wmf    A graphic in Windows Metafile format.

.wp     A document produced by OfficeWriter or WordPerfect.

.wpg    A graphic produced by WordPerfect.

.*wri*    A document produced by Write. Double-click on the file to run Write on it.

.wrk    A spreadsheet produced by Lotus Symphony.

.wrt    A document produced by MacWrite.

.wrd    A document produced by Microsoft Word.

.ws     A document produced by WordStar.

.xbm    A graphic format for the X window system. Primarily used under Unix.

.xcl    A spreadsheet produced by Microsoft Excel.

.xls    A spreadsheet produced by Microsoft Excel.

.xwd    A graphic format for the X window system. Primarily used under Unix.

.**xxe**    An xxencoded file. Use XferPro to decode it. If you use the File Manager to associate XferPro with .*xxe* files, you'll be able to run XferPro on those files by double-clicking on them.

.z      An archive produced by Pack or by GNU Zip. In the case of GNU Zip, files in this format are incompatible with programs like WinZip that know how to process standard .*zip* files.

.Z      A compressed file produced by compress. Primarily used under Unix.

.**zip**    A compressed archive produced by PKZip or a compatible program (e.g., WinZip). Use Win-Zip to extract the files or otherwise manipulate the archive. If you use the File Manager to associate WinZip with *.zip* files, you'll be able to run WinZip on those archives by double-clicking on them.

.zoo    A compressed archive produced by zoo.

# Net File Extensions (by Category)

Appendix A summarizes the typical meanings of a plethora of file extensions commonly encountered on the Net. This appendix presents the same information as Appendix A, but it groups related file extensions together. To find all extensions that indicate archives, for example, just look under "Archives," and to see all the extensions that indicate graphics files, look up "Graphics Files."

As in Appendix A, extensions in boldface indicate files you can manipulate using the software provided with this book, and extensions in italics indicate files you can manipulate using standard Windows programs. For the full story on how to interpret the information that follows, consult the prefatory material at the beginning of Appendix A.

## Archives

.arc   A compressed archive produced by ARC. Use WinZip in conjunction with one of the DOS programs that reads ARC archives to extract the files. (Such programs are described in Chapter 4.) To add files to ARC archives, you'll need a copy of the ARC program. If you use the File Manager to associate WinZip with *.arc* files, you'll be able to run WinZip on those archives by double-clicking on them.

**.arj** A compressed archive produced by ARJ. Use WinZip or ARJ to extract the files or otherwise manipulate the archive. If you use the File Manager to associate WinZip with *.arj* files, you'll be able to run WinZip on those archives by double-clicking on them.

.cpt An archive produced by Compact Pro. Primarily used on the Mac.

.dd A compressed archive produced by Disk Doubler; used on the Mac.

.gz A compressed archive in GNU Zip format. Primarily used under Unix. Don't be fooled by the similar names: files in this format are not compatible with programs like WinZip that know how to process standard *.zip* files.

.hpk A compressed archive produced by HPack.

.hqx An archive produced by BinHex. Primarily used on the Mac.

**.lzh** A compressed archive produced by LHA. Use WinZip or LHA to extract the files or otherwise manipulate the archive. If you use the File Manager to associate WinZip with *.lzh* files, you'll be able to run WinZip on those archives by double-clicking on them.

.pak A compressed archive produced by Pak.

.pit      An archive produced by PackIt. Primarily used on the Mac.

.sea      A self-extracting archive for the Mac.

.shar      A textual archive produced by shar. Used primarily under Unix.

.sit      An archive produced by StuffIt; primarily used on the Mac.

.sqz      A compressed archive produced by Squeeze.

.tar      An archive produced by tar. Primarily used under Unix.

.z      An archive produced by Pack or by GNU Zip. In the case of GNU Zip, files in this format are incompatible with programs like WinZip that know how to process standard *.zip* files.

**.zip**      A compressed archive produced by PKZip or a compatible program (e.g., WinZip). Use Win-Zip to extract the files or otherwise manipulate the archive. If you use the File Manager to associate WinZip with *.zip* files, you'll be able to run WinZip on those archives by double-clicking on them.

.zoo      A compressed archive produced by zoo.

## Documents

.doc      In the context of Windows, this usually indicates a document created with Microsoft Word, but it can also indicate a document created with FrameMaker.

.dox      A document produced by MultiMate.

*.hlp*    If designed for Windows, a Windows help file. Double-click on the file to start the help system on it. If not designed for Windows (e.g., if designed for DOS), often a text file you can read with Notepad.

.html    A document in the hypertext markup language. Used by the World-Wide Web, a tool for accessing information on the Internet.

.rtf     A document in Rich Text Format. Some word processors (e.g., Microsoft Word, FrameMaker) can display these files correctly.

.sgml    A document in Standard Generalized Markup Language (SGML). This format is an emerging standard, and it is likely that full-featured word processors will eventually be able to read such files and display them correctly.

.tex     A document written using TeX typesetting commands. You'll need the TeX software (available for free downloading from the Internet— look for CTAN, the Comprehensive TeX Archive Network) to produce the formatted document.

.w51     A document produced by WordPerfect 5.1.

.wp      A document produced by OfficeWriter or WordPerfect.

*.wri*    A document produced by Write. Double-click on the file to run Write on it.

.wrt     A document produced by MacWrite.

.wrd     A document produced by Microsoft Word.

.ws      A document produced by WordStar.

## Encoded Files

**.mme**   A MIME-encoded file. Use XferPro to decode it. If you use the File Manager to associate Xfer-Pro with *.mme* files, you'll be able to run Xfer-Pro on those files by double-clicking on them.

**.uu**   A uuencoded file. Use XferPro to decode it. If you use the File Manager to associate XferPro with *.uu* files, you'll be able to run XferPro on those files by double-clicking on them.

**.uue**   A uuencoded file. Use XferPro to decode it. If you use the File Manager to associate XferPro with *.uue* files, you'll be able to run XferPro on those files by double-clicking on them.

**.xxe**   An xxencoded file. Use XferPro to decode it. If you use the File Manager to associate XferPro with *.xxe* files, you'll be able to run XferPro on those files by double-clicking on them.

## Executable Files

*.bat*   A DOS batch file. This is an executable file, but it's also textual, so you can use Notepad to view or edit it. To run the file, double-click on it.

*.com*   An executable DOS file. To run the file, double-click on it.

*.exe*   An executable file, typically a program, but sometimes a self-extracting archive. To run the file, double-click on it.

## Graphics Files

.ai   A graphic produced by Adobe Illustrator.

.bit   A monochrome bitmap from a PC.

**.bmp**   A color bitmap for Windows or OS/2. Use LView Pro to view or edit it. If you use the File Manager to associate LView Pro with *.bmp* files, you'll be able to run LView Pro on those files by double-clicking on them.

.cdr    A graphic produced by Corel Draw.

.cgm    A graphics metafile.

.cmu    A graphic produced by the Unix-based CMU Window Manager.

.drw    A graphic produced by either Macdraw or Micrographx Draw. To make things interesting, the two programs write their files in different formats.

.dxf    A graphic produced by AutoCAD.

.eps    A graphic in encapsulated PostScript format.

.epsf   A graphic in encapsulated PostScript format.

**.gif**   An image in GIF format. Use LView Pro to view or edit it. If you use the File Manager to associate LView Pro with *.gif* files, you'll be able to run LView Pro on those files by double-clicking on them.

.img    A graphic produced by GEM Paint.

**.jpg**   An image in JPEG format. Use LView Pro to view or edit it. If you use the File Manager to associate LView Pro with *.jpg* files, you'll be able to run LView Pro on those files by double-clicking on them.

.lbm    A graphic produced by Deluxe Paint.

.mac    A bitmap format for the Mac.

.*msp*    A graphic. Double-click on the file to run Paint-brush on it.

.pbm    A graphical bitmap in Portable Bitmap format. Used primarily under Unix.

.*pcc*    A graphic. Use Paintbrush to view or edit it.

.*pcx*    A graphic. Double-click on the file to run Paint-brush on it.

.pgm    A greyscale graphic produced by PBMPLUS.

.pic    A graphic produced by Lotus 1-2-3, Paul Mace Pictor, or Grasp.

.ppm    A color graphic produced by PBMPLUS.

.ras    A raster image format for Sun workstations.

.rle    A graphic format for raster images.

**.tga**    An image in TrueVision Targa format. Use LView Pro to view or edit it. If you use the File Manager to associate LView Pro with .*tga* files, you'll be able to run LView Pro on those files by double-clicking on them.

.tif    A graphic in TIFF format.

.tiff    A graphic in TIFF format.

.win    A graphic produced by TrueVision Targa.

.wmf    A graphic in Windows Metafile format.

.wpg    A graphic produced by WordPerfect.

.xbm    A graphic format for the X window system. Primarily used under Unix.

.xwd    A graphic format for the X window system. Primarily used under Unix.

# Movies

.avi  A movie in Video for Windows format. If you have the appropriate MCI device driver installed, you can double-click on the file to run Windows' Media Player on it.

**.mpg**  A movie in MPEG format. Use the MPEGView program DMFW to view it. If you use the File Manager to associate DMFW with *.mpg* files, you'll be able to watch them by double-clicking on them. If DMFW provides unsatisfactory performance, you may wish to view MPEG movies under DOS; see Chapter 6 for details on how to do it.

# Print Files

.dvi  A "device-independent" version of a document that's been prepared for printing in general, but has not yet been prepared for a particular printer. Produced by the TeX typesetting system. Primarily used under Unix.

.hpgl  A file prepared for plotting on an HP plotter.

.pcl  A file prepared for printing on an HP Laserjet printer.

.ps  A document or image in PostScript format, which is designed for printers. Primarily used under Unix. You'll need a PostScript previewer (available for free downloading from the Internet—look for a program called Ghostscript) or a PostScript printer to see the document or the image.

## Programs

.c      A program written in the C programming language.

.C      A program written in the C++ programming language. This extension is primarily used under Unix.

.cc     A program written in the C++ programming language.

.cpp    A program written in the C++ programming language.

.cxx    A program written in the C++ programming language.

.h      A header file for a program written in the C or C++ programming languages.

## Sound Files

**.au**   A sound file for Sun, DEC, and NExT workstations. Use WPLAny to listen to it. If you use the File Manager to associate WPLAny with *.au* files, you'll be able to listen to them by double-clicking on them.

**.iff**  A sound file for the Amiga. Use WPLAny to listen to it. If you use the File Manager to associate WPLAny with *.iff* files, you'll be able to listen to them by double-clicking on them.

.mid    A MIDI sound file. If you have the appropriate MCI device driver installed, you can double-click on the file to run Windows' Media Player on it.

**.snd**  A sound file for Sounder/Soundtools. Use WPLAny to listen to it. If you use the File Manager to associate WPLAny with *.snd* files, you'll be able to listen to them by double-clicking on them.

.snd  A sound file for the Macintosh.

**.voc**  A sound file for DOS. Use WPLAny to listen to it. If you use the File Manager to associate WPLAny with *.voc* files, you'll be able to listen to them by double-clicking on them.

**.wav**  A sound file for Windows. Use WPLAny to listen to it. If you use the File Manager to associate WPLAny with *.wav* files, you'll be able to listen to them by double-clicking on them. You can use the Sound Recorder that comes with Windows to edit *.wav* files; see Chapter 6 for information on how to do it.

## Spreadsheets

.csv  A spreadsheet represented as comma-separated values.

.syl  A spreadsheet in Microsoft SYLK format.

.wk1  A spreadsheet in Lotus 1-2-3 format.

.wk2  A spreadsheet in Lotus 1-2-3 format.

.wk3  A spreadsheet in Lotus 1-2-3 format.

.wrk  A spreadsheet produced by Lotus Symphony.

.xcl  A spreadsheet produced by Microsoft Excel.

.xls  A spreadsheet produced by Microsoft Excel.

## Text Files

.1st   Usually used as the extension of a documentation file you should read immediately after extracting the contents of an archive, e.g.., *readme.1st*. Use Notepad to view or edit the file.

.asc   A text file in ASCII format. Use Notepad to view or edit the file.

.doc   In the context of DOS or Unix, this usually indicates a text file, typically documentation for an accompanying program. Use Notepad to view or edit the file.

.lst   A textual listing of some type. Use Notepad to view or edit the file.

.me   Usually used as the extension of a README file, i.e., *read.me*. Use Notepad to view or edit the file.

.txt   A text file. Use Notepad to view or edit it.

## Other File Types

.bin   A binary file. Such files are almost never portable from one kind of computer to another.

.dbf   A file produced by dBASE.

.dll   A Windows dynamically linked library file.

.fax   As Bernard Aboba puts it in his *Online User's Encyclopedia*, this indicates a file in "one of dozens of incompatible fax formats."

.image   A file containing an exact binary image of a Macintosh disk.

.Z   A compressed file produced by compress. Primarily used under Unix.

# Index